HOLLYWOOD MYTHS

The Shocking Truths Behind Film's
Most Incredible Secrets and Scandals

JOE WILLIAMS

Voyageur Press

First published in 2012 by Voyageur Press, an imprint of MBI Publishing Company, 400 First Avenue North, Suite 300, Minneapolis, MN 55401 USA

© 2012 Voyageur Press

Voyageur Press titles are also available at discounts in bulk quantity for industrial or sales-promotional use. For details write to Special Sales Manager at MBI Publishing Company, 400 First Avenue North, Suite 300, Minneapolis, MN 55401 USA.

To find out more about our books, visit us online at www.voyageurpress.com.

ISBN: 978-0-7603-4241-1

Library of Congress Cataloging-in-Publication Data

Williams, Joe, 1958-
 Hollywood myths : the shocking truths behind film's most incredible secrets and scandals / Joe Williams.
   p. cm.
 Includes index.
 Summary: "In Hollywood myths, veteran film critic Joe Williams dissects the film industry's biggest myths and rumors, from the dawn of the silver screen to the twenty-first century. Myths discussed pertain to superstars, power couples, groundbreaking films, and the industry itself"-- Provided by publisher.
 ISBN 978-0-7603-4241-1
 1. Motion picture actors and actresses--California--Los Angeles--Biography. 2. Motion picture industry--California--Los Angeles--Anecdotes. 3. Scandals--California--Los Angeles. I. Title.
 PN1998.2W49 2012
 791.4309794'94--dc23
                          2012008080

Editors: Dennis Pernu and Grace Labatt
Design manager: Cindy Samargia Laun
Layout: Pauline Molinari
Cover designer: John Barnett

Printed in China

10 9 8 7 6 5 4 3 2 1

To Kathryn

Contents

INTRODUCTION 6

PART 1
Legendary Stars 10
1. Charlie Chaplin 12
2. Rudolph Valentino 16
3. Roscoe "Fatty" Arbuckle 20
4. Jean Harlow 24
5. John Wayne 28
6. Humphrey Bogart 32
7. Montgomery Clift 36
8. Marlon Brando 40
9. Jerry Lewis 46
10. Elvis Presley 49
11. Woody Allen 52
12. Harrison Ford 56
13. Arnold Schwarzenegger 59
14. Eddie Murphy 63
15. Tom Cruise 66

PART 2
Odd Couples 70
16. Fred Astaire and Ginger Rogers 72
17. Spencer Tracy and Katharine Hepburn 75
18. Bob Hope and Bing Crosby 79
19. Cary Grant and Randolph Scott 82
20. Rock Hudson and Jim Nabors 86
21. Elizabeth Taylor and Richard Burton 90
22. Brad Pitt and Angelina Jolie 96

PART 3
The Final Curtain 100
23. Peg Entwistle 102
24. James Dean 105
25. George Reeves 109
26. Carl Switzer 112
27. Marilyn Monroe 116
28. Sharon Tate 124

29. Sal Mineo 128
30. Jean Seberg 132
31. Jayne Mansfield 135
32. Natalie Wood 138
33. John Belushi 142
34. Heath Ledger 146

PART 4
Mythic Movies 150
35. *The Great Train Robbery* 152
36. *The Birth of a Nation* 154
37. *The Jazz Singer* 158
38. *The Wizard of Oz* 161
39. *Gone With the Wind* 167
40. *Citizen Kane* 171
41. *Casablanca* 174
42. *It's a Wonderful Life* 178
43. *The Graduate* 182
44. *The Godfather* 185
45. *Jaws* 189
46. *Star Wars* 192
47. *Titanic* 196

PART 5
The Movie Industry 200
48. Hollywood, California, USA 202
49. Foreign Markets 206
50. Drive-in Movies 208
51. The Popcorn Business 212
52. The Audience 215
53. The Critics 217
54. The Ratings System 220
55. 3-D 223
56. The Academy Awards 229

Index 238
About the Author 240
Acknowledgments 240

Introduction

Hollywood is built on myths, both on and off the screen. While teams of talented people play make-believe for the cameras, other teams construct stories about the stars, stories that movie buffs consume like popcorn.

For better or worse, many of us learn as much from movies as we do from school. Some of those lessons are extracurricular, drawn from the personal lives of the teachers. We get notions about love from Elizabeth Taylor and Richard Burton, ideas about courage from Bob Hope and Humphrey Bogart, and parables about ambition from Marilyn Monroe and James Dean.

The trick is to separate fact from fiction, a hard task when publicists and professional gossips pull the truth in opposite directions. For every press release about a starlet who was discovered drinking a milkshake at Schwab's Pharmacy, there's a rumor about a floozy who stabbed her abusive boyfriend and forced her daughter to take the rap. (Like so many Hollywood stories, both of those legends about Lana Turner are false. She was discovered at a place called the Top Hat Café, and her daughter Cheryl Crane still swears that she was the one who wielded the blade and saved her mother's life.)

This book is a guide to many of the most popular Hollywood myths—a few of which turn out to be true. Some of these myths involve the lives of legendary stars. Some involve the making of iconic films. And some involve the tenets of the billion-dollar industry itself, which is barely one hundred years old and is still evolving alongside taste and technology.

In the Internet era, myths spread at the speed of light, perpetuated by people who don't always check multiple sources.

But I do.

As the film critic for the daily *St. Louis Post-Dispatch* newspaper, I approach movies as both a fan and a journalist. I have reviewed more than two thousand films, interviewed many of the stars who are mentioned in this book, and attended every Academy Awards ceremony since the reign of *Gladiator*. I've ridden in a limousine with O. J. and Nicole Simpson, traded conspiracy theories with Oliver Stone, and shared a cookie with Marisa Tomei.

Following page: The Star Mural near Hollywood Boulevard in Los Angeles, by Thomas Suriya.
© Art Kowalsky/Alamy

Before I was a film reviewer, I traveled west on Route 66 in the same migration as my college classmates Brad Pitt and Sheryl Crow. In Hollywood, I worked as a movie extra, a set painter, and a rock critic.

In both my personal and professional lives, I've confronted one of the biggest Hollywood myths of all: the notion that success in the film industry is a matter of luck. In my experience, most of the people in the movie business are intelligent, talented, and hard-working professionals who have rightly earned their success. Like wealthy, attractive people elsewhere, movie stars enjoy their privileges, but most of them are not the depraved fiends that scandal-mongers make them out to be.

In this book, you won't find gossip about the heartthrob who had a tryst with a rodent (because it's not true) or the second-generation star who was born a hermaphrodite (because even if it were true, it would expose a living person to needless ridicule). For such scuttlebutt there are countless online resources of varying value. The conscientious website snopes.com is a good place to start exploring urban legends, findadeath. com includes some ghoulishly good information about celebrity demise, and Wikipedia is roughly as accurate as *Encyclopedia Britannica* for the basic facts.

Because so many Golden Age movie stars have ridden into the sunset and the truth about old Hollywood is buried beneath layers of legend, no anthology like this one can pretend to be definitive. But I hope and believe that most of this material is more accurate than the conventional wisdom.

If you have your own Hollywood secrets to share, I invite you to join the conversation. You can write to me at hollywoodmyths@gmail.com. Better yet, you can write your own book and then sell the rights. Maybe the film version will win an award, and on the Oscar podium you can feed the myth that you never dreamed such a thing was possible.

—*Joe Williams*
St. Louis, Missouri, USA

PART 1

Legendary
STARS

CHARLIE CHAPLIN

Was the Little Tramp the legitimate king of the silent-film era?

You can say a lot of things about Charlie Chaplin: that he had a weakness for teenage girls, that he fathered eleven (or possibly twelve) children, that he was forced from his adopted country by the FBI. But be careful about saying that the comic genius was the undisputed king of the silent-movie era.

In popularity and prestige, the Little Tramp was often number one, but for most of the 1920s Chaplin shared the spotlight with his swashbuckling friend Douglas Fairbanks; Fairbanks' sweetheart Mary Pickford; "It Girl" Clara Bow; matinee idols Rudolph Valentino and John Gilbert; cowboys William S. Hart and Tom Mix; fellow comedians Buster Keaton, Fatty Arbuckle, and Harold Lloyd; and even canine star Rin Tin Tin. Yet in the past century, history has done Chaplin some favors that weren't bestowed on the others.

After arriving in California in 1913 at the age of twenty-four, the London-born vaudevillian made more than eighty films, many of them one-reelers, for Mack Sennett, the producer of the Keystone Kops comedies. Chaplin invented the Tramp character for his second film, creating his signature look by combining too-big trousers originally owned by Arbuckle, a too-small derby from Arbuckle's father-in-law, a cutaway coat from comedian Chester Conklin, size-fourteen shoes from comedian Ford Sterling (which Chaplin wore on the wrong feet), and a crepe-hair mustache from Sennett's make-up department. (The bamboo cane was Chaplin's own.)

The courtly, resourceful vagabond was an immediate sensation, particularly with the new immigrants who cheered every time he outwitted an ornery cop or snooty socialite. The decidedly non-American character

Charlie Chaplin's Little Tramp character was down on his luck; his creator, on the other hand, was a brilliant comic who had luck on his side. *Hulton Archive/ Stringer/Getty Image*

also helped popularize movies overseas. Chaplin soon became the highest-paid performer in Hollywood and arguably the most famous man in the world. He started his own studio in a mock-Tudor complex he built at Sunset Boulevard and La Brea (later to become the headquarters of A&M Records, where "We Are the World" was recorded). In 1919, Chaplin, Fairbanks, Pickford, and director D. W. Griffith formed the distribution company United Artists, asserting their independence from the moguls who initially didn't even list actors' names in the movie credits. (United Artists, which continues to operate as a specialty studio, was briefly co-owned by Tom Cruise until it was recently reacquired by MGM.)

And here's where history favors Chaplin. While he (and to a lesser extent his UA partners, whose careers had already peaked) had artistic control over his movies, other silent stars saw their movies hacked to pieces—figuratively, by studio chiefs who edited the films to suit their own tastes, and then literally, by recyclers who used the celluloid for guitar picks or as a cheap source of silver. In the old days, movies were shot on highly combustible silver-nitrate film stock. The advent of sound circa 1927 made silent movies a worthless commodity taking up space on studio shelves. It is estimated that 80 percent of silent films were destroyed. Many were burned. Those that weren't melted down for their minerals were likely to deteriorate on their own unless the reels were stored in a cool, dry place.

Chaplin, however, controlled and preserved his negatives. And because he was so popular internationally, some of his pre-UA output has been found in cold storage in far-reaching places like the Yukon and Russia. Modern audiences who have never heard of Fatty Arbuckle or William S. Hart can therefore still see and enjoy Charlie Chaplin's movies. And thus they overestimate his market dominance.

Another factor benefiting Chaplin's status is that many of his best-known films were actually made after "talkies" had been invented. On both an artistic and technical level, *The Circus* (1928), *City Lights* (1931), *Modern Times* (1936), and *The Great Dictator* (1940) are superior to the silent films of the teens and early 1920s. Those early movies were sometimes shot with hand-cranked cameras, and if they were ever shown to later audiences, the speed was not corrected for modern projectors. Except for some comedies, like the Keystone Kops one-reelers, silent movies were not as herky-jerky as many people now believe.

A final fluke of history is that the person who tried hardest to destroy Chaplin's reputation was a self-righteous hypocrite.

Although Chaplin helped sell war bonds during World War I, some in Washington resented that he never applied for American citizenship. When the postwar prosperity of the Roaring '20s—which roared with particular might in Hollywood—produced a backlash against a seeming lack of morals and propriety, FBI director J. Edgar Hoover determined to clean up the entertainment industry. He decided that the best way to do this would be to target the industry's most visible symbol.

Chaplin made an ideal scapegoat. In his heyday, he married and divorced two teenagers: actress Mildred Harris (with whom he had a son who died young) and waitress-turned-actress Lita Murray (whom Chaplin met when she was twelve, married when she was sixteen, and expensively divorced after the birth of their two sons). He had rumored affairs with actresses Pola Negri, Louise Brooks, and Marion Davies. (Chaplin was with Davies and her benefactor William Randolph Hearst on the night when director Thomas Ince mysteriously died aboard Hearst's yacht. The 2001 Peter Bogdanovich movie *The Cat's Meow* speculates that Hearst mistook Ince for Chaplin and shot him out of jealousy.) It was never entirely clear when or even if Chaplin legally married his longtime companion Paulette Godard. Chaplin was also dragged into a paternity suit by actress Joan Barry, whom he was forced to compensate even though blood tests proved he was not the father of the infant girl in question.

After the stock market crash of 1929 and the ensuing Great Depression, Chaplin's movies became more overtly sympathetic to the downtrodden. Although *The Great Dictator* was a brave and timely denunciation of Chaplin-lookalike Adolf Hitler, Hoover branded the actor a communist. Chaplin was called before the House Un-American Activities Committee but never testified. (He did, however, send the committee a statement denying he had ever been a member of any political party.) In 1952, when Chaplin sailed back to the United States from the London premiere of the semi-autobiographical talkie *Limelight*, immigration officials forbade his reentry on moral and political grounds.

Chaplin did not return to the United States until almost a quarter century later, when he was given an honorary Oscar and the longest standing ovation in the history of the event: twelve minutes. By then, Hoover had been dead for more than three years, and rumors had leaked that the crime-fighting bachelor had been a Mafia apologist, gambling addict, and closeted homosexual. (As documented in Clint Eastwood's 2011 film *J. Edgar*, Hoover was inseparable from his lieutenant Clyde Tolson.)

Charlie Chaplin died at his home in Switzerland on Christmas Day 1977, two years after being made a Knight Commander of the British Empire by Queen Elizabeth II. He and his wife Oona (daughter of playwright Eugene O'Neill), whom he married when he was fifty-four and she was eighteen, had eight children, including actress Geraldine Chaplin.

Even in death, Chaplin wasn't allowed to rest in peace. In 1978, his casket and body were exhumed and held for ransom. Three months later, police arrested an unemployed Polish auto mechanic for the crime and Chaplin was reburied in a more secure Swiss vault. ★

RUDOLPH VALENTINO

Was the silent star a simpering sissy?

With apologies to Tom Cruise, Rudolph Valentino may be the most misunderstood superstar in film history. Today he is caricatured as a Latin lover who could not have survived the transition to the sound era. And indeed, his sudden death in 1926 at age thirty-one roughly coincided with the end of the silent era.

But Valentino may have been the first rebel of cinema. He fought against typecasting and against journalists who questioned his masculinity. He even founded and awarded a precursor to the Oscars, to honor excellence in the young art form of film.

Rodolfo Alfonzo Raffaello Pierre Filibert Guglielmi di Valentina D'Antonguolla was born in 1895 in Castellaneta, Puglia, Italy, a city in the heel of the boot-shaped nation. Valentino did not speak a word of English when he arrived at Ellis Island in 1913, but he was not a bumpkin. His father had been a veterinarian, and Rudolph had spent a year in Paris after earning a degree from an agricultural school.

Rudolph Valentino in The Young Rajah, 1922. Time & Life Pictures/Getty Images

In New York he found a job as a "taxi dancer," entertaining wealthy women in nightclubs. One of them was a Chilean heiress who dragged him into her much-publicized divorce trial (and eventually murdered her husband). Valentino fled west with a musical troupe, then briefly worked in a theatrical production for Al Jolson that took him to Los Angeles. In Hollywood, Valentino taught dance, played small roles in a few films—often

as the villain—and impulsively married actress Jean Acker, a lesbian who locked him out of her bedroom on their wedding night.

Frustrated by a loveless marriage and a stalled career, Valentino returned to the East Coast. During a stop in Florida he read and saw the film potential in the novel *The Four Horsemen of the Apocalypse* by Spanish author Vicente Blasco Ibáñez. When Valentino reached New York he sought out the production company that owned the rights to the book and was wise to have done so—the producers cast him in the film, which became one of the biggest hits of the silent era.

On the set of his next film, he met and fell in love with art director Natacha Rambova. An avant-garde bisexual, Rambova was an important influence on Valentino's image and career choices as he starred in hit films such as *The Sheik* (1921) and *Blood and Sand* (1922). At a succession of studios, Valentino's salary and creative demands escalated. In 1922 he divorced Acker and tried to marry Rambova in Mexico, but was briefly jailed for bigamy because he had not waited a full year, as required by law.

> *"Women are not in love with me but with the picture of me on the screen. I am merely the canvas on which women paint their dreams."*
>
> — Rudolph Valentino

When the Famous Players-Lasky Corporation studio refused to let Valentino film his next movie in Europe, where he hoped to reunite with the family he had not seen in ten years, he went on a one-man strike. He also went on a cross-country dance tour with Rambova, sponsored by a makeup company, and at every stop he denounced the studio, sometimes on the radio. (Around this time he also recorded two songs, one in English and one in Spanish, belying the myth that he had a high, unpleasant voice. You can hear his heavily accented baritone in clips that have been uploaded to the Internet.)

Partly because it had cut its tie with scandal-plagued superstar Fatty Arbuckle, the foundering studio relented, increasing Valentino's salary from $1,250 to $7,500 per week and granting him creative control over his films. He married Rambova, fulfilled his contract, and traveled with his wife to Europe to accumulate authentic costumes for future projects.

In 1925, Valentino created the Rudolph Valentino Medal, arguably the first award to recognize artistic achievement in film. The inaugural winner of the juried competition, for which Valentino declared himself ineligible, was John Barrymore for *Beau Brummel*.

Valentino wouldn't live to see a second presentation.

The star was offered a $10,000-per-week contract with United Artists, the company that had been founded by Charlie Chaplin, Mary Pickford, Douglas Fairbanks, and D. W. Griffith six years earlier. There was a stipulation, however: the meddlesome Rambova was not to be allowed on set. Valentino agreed to the deal, and soon he and Rambova bitterly divorced.

Valentino's films for UA did not generate the money or magic of *The Sheik*, and he suffered a backlash in the tabloid press. A 1926 column in the *Chicago Tribune* blamed Valentino for the feminization of the American male. The writer noted that the actor had inspired the vogue of slicked-back hair, that he had been associated with a makeup company, and that, because of his influence, the men's room in a swank Chicago hotel had installed an automated face-powder dispenser.

Notwithstanding what some posthumous books assert, there is no reliable evidence that Rudolph Valentino was gay. There is no question, however, that the assault on his manhood enraged him. Valentino challenged the *Tribune* writer to a boxing match but got no response. However, the boxing reporter for the *New York Evening Journal* volunteered to fight the actor. Valentino trained with champion boxer Jack Dempsey, and on the roof of Manhattan's Ambassador Hotel, the sheik defeated the scribe.

On August 16 of that year, at the same hotel, Valentino collapsed from appendicitis and ulcers and was hospitalized. As word spread, hundreds of fans gathered on the sidewalk below his room. He died on August 23, 1926.

Valentino's New York funeral attracted 100,000 mourners and incited a riot. Actress Pola Negri, declaring she had been secretly engaged to Valentino, fainted beside his coffin. A black-shirted legion saluted the star, claiming to be fascist emissaries of Italian leader Benito Mussolini. (They were actually actors hired by the funeral home as a publicity stunt.) Several fans around the world committed suicide.

The body was shipped to California, where Valentino was mourned by 80,000 fans and buried in a crypt at the Hollywood Memorial Park Cemetery.

Every year on the anniversary of his death, one or more mysterious women in black lay red roses at Valentino's grave. A Hollywood publicist claimed that the first woman was an actress he had hired, although the family of a woman named Marquesa de Lara claimed that she was the original mourner and had been Valentino's illicit lover. De Lara's daughter has led the annual charade since her mother's death in 1973. ★

ROSCOE "FATTY" ARBUCKLE

Was the rotund comedian a killer?

Fatty was framed.

Although silent-film comedian Roscoe "Fatty" Arbuckle was charged in the death of a starlet, he was never convicted, and a jury declared that he was owed a public apology. That didn't stop the tabloid press from crucifying him, however, and the myth of his complicity has endured.

Roscoe Arbuckle weighed at least fourteen pounds when he was born in Smith Center, Kansas, in 1887. His mother died when he was twelve, and his father abandoned him soon after. Eventually, he made his way to California, where the shy, rotund Roscoe became a graceful stage comedian and was tagged with the nickname "Fatty."

In 1909, he married an aspiring actress named Minta Durfee and embarked on a series of vaudeville tours of East Asia. When he returned in 1913, he was hired by Mack Sennett's fledgling Keystone Studios for its Keystone Kops shorts. There, Arbuckle became the first film performer to take a pie in the face. Those ten-minute movies, many directed by Arbuckle himself and some featuring a newcomer named Charlie Chaplin, proved so popular that Arbuckle started his own production company.

Arbuckle was lured away by Paramount, which offered him a million dollars per year and the chance to make feature films. By the early 1920s, he was starring in six movies a year. For Labor Day weekend, 1921, he

Before the infamous Labor Day, 1921, weekend, 300-pound comedian "Fatty" Arbuckle was making $1 million a year and sometimes juggling three films at a time. *Hulton Archive/Getty Images*

decided a vacation was in order, so Arbuckle and a director named Fred Fischbach planned a drive to San Francisco. Arbuckle suffered a serious burn to his backside while getting his car repaired and wanted to cancel the trip, but Fischbach fatefully convinced him otherwise.

Arbuckle, Fischbach, and their actor friend Lowell Sherman checked into three adjoining rooms at San Francisco's St. Francis Hotel. On September 5 there was an impromptu party in their suite. Among the uninvited guests drinking the bootleg liquor were an actress named Virginia Rappe and her friend, Bambina Maude Delmont.

Rappe had played bit parts in movies and had been acquainted with Arbuckle for five years, but her career never took off. She'd had a troubled childhood, at least five illegal abortions, and an out-of-wedlock baby she put up for adoption. Like other struggling actresses of the era, Rappe might have supplemented her income with prostitution, which may explain the presence of Delmont, a convicted forger and extortionist who used her female friends to lure rich men into compromising situations.

On that afternoon, Arbuckle intended to go sightseeing with a friend named Mae Taub, the daughter of prohibitionist preacher Billy Sunday. When Arbuckle went to his room to change clothes, he found Rappe vomiting in the bathroom. He moved her to his bed and went to another room to dress. When he returned, Rappe had fallen off the bed. He picked her up and daubed her with ice from a bucket, perhaps to see if she had fainted or was merely faking. Rappe began screaming and tearing at her clothes, something she had done during previous drunken binges. Several party guests entered the room.

Arbuckle and Fischbach placed Rappe in a bathtub to cool off, then moved her to a separate room on the same floor. Arbuckle called the hotel manager and doctor to check on the woman, whom he thought was merely drunk, then he proceeded with his sightseeing trip. Arbuckle checked out of the hotel and returned to Los Angeles the next day.

A few days later, on September 9, Rappe died. The official cause of death was a ruptured bladder.

The tabloid press, led by William Randolph Hearst's *San Francisco Examiner*, claimed that Arbuckle had raped the helpless girl and that his massive girth had caused her organs to explode. Although there were no signs of an assault—three different doctors examined her for evidence—and plenty of signs that Rappe had chronic health problems, Arbuckle was charged with manslaughter. He was prosecuted by a district attorney named Matthew Brady, who intended to run for governor on a law-and-order platform.

An unwavering Arbuckle testified, with his estranged wife, Durfee, and many fans in attendance, and the jury favored acquittal by a vote of ten to two. A mistrial was declared because of the deadlock.

At the second trial, two prosecution witnesses recanted their original testimony. This time the jury leaned toward conviction but remained dead-locked, resulting in another mistrial.

For the third trial, Arbuckle's attorney mounted a fierce defense. Some prosecution witnesses admitted that they had been strong-armed by Brady; one fled the country. After Arbuckle's testimony, the jury needed just one minute to declare him not guilty and another five minutes to draft an unprecedented statement of apology. It read:

> *Acquittal is not enough for Roscoe Arbuckle. We feel that a great injustice has been done him. We feel also that it was only our plain duty to give him this exoneration, under the evidence, for there was not the slightest proof adduced to connect him in any way with the commission of a crime.*
>
> *He was manly throughout the case, and told a straightforward story on the witness stand, which we all believed.*
>
> *The happening at the hotel was an unfortunate affair for which Arbuckle, so the evidence shows, was in no way responsible.*
>
> *We wish him success, and hope that the American people will take the judgment of fourteen men and women who have sat listening for thirty-one days to evidence, that Roscoe Arbuckle is entirely innocent and free from all blame.*

Yet immediately after his acquittal, Arbuckle was banned from making movies by Hollywood's official censor, William H. Hays, the former U.S. postmaster general hired by the studios to improve their reputations. Arbuckle's movies were pulled from theaters. Although the ban lasted less than a year, the damage was done. In the scandal-plagued early 1920s, when director William Desmond Taylor was mysteriously murdered and a matinee idol named Wallace Reid died from morphine addiction, the studios did not want to be associated with Fatty Arbuckle.

Eventually, working under the pseudonym William Goodrich, Arbuckle was allowed to direct some silent films, including a few with his loyal friend and one-time protégé Buster Keaton. But Arbuckle started drinking heavily, and his wife divorced him in 1925.

After the trials, it took ten years for Arbuckle to appear again on camera. He had roles in a few short talkies with "Stooge" Shemp Howard, and in June 1933, Arbuckle signed a deal to star in a feature film for Warner Bros. But on the night when he celebrated the contract—and his first anniversary with his new wife—Arbuckle died in his sleep at age forty-six. ★

4

JEAN HARLOW

Was the platinum blonde complicit in murder?

The short life of Jean Harlow, the first sex symbol of talking pictures, was punctuated by an unspeakable crime and its cover-up.

Just two months after Harlow married producer Paul Bern in 1932, he was found shot to death in their Beverly Hills home. Bern was a kindly German immigrant who, at age forty-two, was twice as old as his actress bride. A note near his lifeless, naked body suggested that Bern's "abject humiliation" had led him to commit suicide. Soon the rumor spread that the source of Bern's humiliation was impotence.

But Paul Bern had been murdered.

Bern had made the bubbly blonde Harlow a star. She was born Harlean Carpenter in Kansas City, Missouri, in 1911. The daughter of a dentist and an aspiring actress, young Harlean attended private schools, including one near Chicago where she met a rich kid named Charles McGrew. They eloped when she was sixteen and moved to Hollywood, where Carpenter had spent part of her childhood while her mother tried to make it in show business. There the couple established themselves as hard-partying socialites.

On a dare from an actress friend, Harlean Carpenter registered with Central Casting under her mother's maiden name, Jean Harlow. Soon the newly christened actress was performing bit parts in silent films. She signed a five-year contract with Hal Roach Studios, which cast her in three Laurel & Hardy movies, but she begged out of the contract when McGrew objected to his wife working.

The elder Jean Harlow returned to California with a new husband, a ne'er-do-well named Marino Bello. When the two of them started aggressively pushing younger Jean's career, McGrew filed for an annulment.

"The Original Blonde Bombshell" caused a boom in the peroxide business. Photograph from 1933, four years before Harlow's untimely death.
George Hurrell/Stringer/ Getty Images

With prodding from her mother and Bello, Jean caught the eye of some powerful men, including gangster Abner "Longie" Zwillman and movie mogul Howard Hughes. Hughes was in the process of converting his 1930 aviation epic *Hell's Angels* from a silent film to a talkie (incorporating technology that became available midway through production), and he needed an English-speaking substitute for silent film star Greta Nissen, who had a strong Norwegian accent. Jean Harlow, nineteen at the time, won the part.

Soon after Harlow uttered the immortal line "Would you be shocked if I changed into something more comfortable?" the platinum blonde became a red-hot property. Female fans imitated her hair color, which Harlow claimed was her natural shade, but few could mimic her natural sexiness, which she accented with form-fitting satin gowns and a noticeable lack of undergarments.

Bern, a respected producer at MGM, convinced the studio to buy Harlow's contract from Hughes and cast her in a 1932 adaptation of the popular novel *Red-Headed Woman*. Harlow was thrilled to be joining MGM's elite stable. She married her benefactor on July 2, 1932.

The studio decided that Harlow's good-time-gal persona would be a perfect onscreen match for rising star Clark Gable. It was while Gable and Harlow were making *Red Dust* that Bern was killed.

On Sunday night, September 4, Bern had a quarrel with Harlow, ostensibly about their new Beverly Hills home, which had been a wedding present from Bern that Harlow reportedly thought was too secluded. The new bride left to have dinner at her mother's.

Sometime later that night, another woman arrived at the Beverly Hills house. It was Dorothy Millette, an aspiring actress with whom Bern had been romantically involved in New York more than a decade earlier. Although they had once been close, Millette was mentally ill, and Bern had put her in a sanitarium. By the time she emerged, seemingly cured of her schizophrenia but unaware of how much time had passed, Bern was working in Hollywood. For many years he rented Millette a room in Manhattan's Algonquin Hotel under the name "Mrs. Paul Bern," but he rebuffed her requests to join him in California, where the middle-aged woman thought she could be an ingénue in the movies he was making.

By the spring of 1932, Millette knew about Bern's affair with Harlow. She threatened to confront them in Hollywood. Bern convinced her to go to San Francisco instead and wait for him to contact her. She stayed for several months at the Plaza Hotel, but by Labor Day weekend, she would not be deterred. So Bern engineered an argument to make his new bride leave the house, then he waited for the arrival of the unstable woman who considered herself to be his common-law wife.

That night, the butler and cook saw a limousine deliver a veiled woman to the house. Later they heard an animated discussion and saw the woman rush off. The next morning the gardener found two champagne glasses and a wet bathing suit by the pool—just before the butler found Bern in the bedroom with a bullet hole in his head.

Instead of calling the police, the butler called MGM. Scandal-averse studio chief Louis B. Mayer, his assistant Irving Thalberg, and security chief Whitey Hendry were all on the scene before the cops. So was a producer named Samuel Marx, a friend of Bern's who had gotten a tip from a journalist with a police scanner. Marx was gently shooed away by Thalberg, yet that was hardly the end of his involvement. Skeptical of Mayer's explanation that Bern was fatally ashamed of his impotence, Marx embarked on a sixty-year informal investigation of the case, which he recounted in his 1990 book *Deadly Illusions*.

The author learned that on the night of Bern's death, an MGM limo had driven a woman away from Bern's house and proceeded directly to San Francisco. The next day, Dorothy Millette checked out of the Plaza Hotel, boarded a steamship on the Sacramento River, and leapt to her death.

Meanwhile, ex-cop Whitey Hendry doctored the crime scene, retrieving the gun from the other side of the room and placing it in Bern's dead hand. He then tore a page from Bern's notebook, which apologized to Harlow for the "comedy" of the forced argument that had driven her away, and set it in the open to look like a suicide note.

Bern's funeral was a star-studded affair, with one of the largest floral arrangements that Hollywood had ever seen. Despite being overcome with grief, Harlow discreetly paid for Millette's lonely funeral in Sacramento and a headstone that read "Dorothy Millette Bern."

Six days after Bern's death, his movie *Grand Hotel* opened in theaters nationwide, with Harlow stealing scenes from legends like John Barrymore and Greta Garbo. It would eventually win the Academy Award for Best Picture.

Harlow completed work on *Red Dust* (1932) and continued to reign as one of the biggest stars in Hollywood. In 1933, to defuse the scandal of her affair with married boxer Max Baer, executives at MGM convinced her to wed cinematographer Harold Rosson. They divorced after seven months.

In 1934, Harlow seemed to find true love at last with actor William Powell. They were secretly engaged for more than two years, but because Powell was in his forties and recently divorced from Carole Lombard, Mayer discouraged them from getting married. While she was waiting for her boss' blessing, Harlow became ill on the set of *Saratoga*. Her mother, a Christian Scientist, refused to take her to a hospital until Powell insisted. Harlow was diagnosed with a kidney ailment, slipped into a coma, and died on June 7, 1937. She was only twenty-six years old.

While a nation of film fans mourned for the fallen star, *Saratoga*, Harlow's sixth film with Gable, was completed with a trio of stand-ins for the scenes Harlow had not yet had the chance to film. Except for the animated *Snow White and the Seven Dwarfs*, it was the biggest hit of the year. ★

5

JOHN WAYNE

Was the cowboy star a hero in real life?

"The Duke" was the ultimate Hollywood hero. But was John Wayne a hero in real life? He was not, and his failure to fight when his country called haunted him the rest of his life.

John Wayne was born Marion Michael Morrison in Winterset, Iowa, in 1907 and raised in the Los Angeles suburb of Glendale. After high school, Wayne applied to the U.S. Naval Academy but was turned down, so he enrolled at the University of Southern California, where he played football. While still in college, he worked in the props department of a movie studio, and he and his Trojan teammates appeared in a couple of silent films. (One of the biggest fans of the USC team was silent film star Clara Bow, but there's no proof to confirm the widely repeated rumor that she slept with several of the players—including Wayne, who suffered a shoulder injury [while body surfing] and was off the team by the time Bow was throwing house parties for them.)

In 1930, when he landed the starring role in the Western talkie *The Big Trail*, the actor was given the stage name "John Wayne" by director Raoul Walsh. The big-budget film was a flop, but it did not derail Wayne's career. He had starring roles in about eighty low-budget "horse operas" over the course of the next decade, including several in which his character sang. (The voice was dubbed.)

Wayne's big breakthrough came in 1939 with *Stagecoach*, the first of more than twenty films he would make with director John Ford. In the film—which was nominated for five Academy Awards and was said to have been watched by Orson Welles more than forty times during the making of *Citizen Kane*—Wayne played the Ringo Kid, a good-hearted gunslinger determined to get revenge for the murder of his father and brother.

After the Japanese bombed Pearl Harbor in December 1941, many Hollywood stars volunteered for military service, including Clark Gable, Henry Fonda, and James Stewart. Cowboy star Gene Autry said it was the duty of big-screen heroes to serve in uniform. But at age thirty-four, with four children at home, Wayne sought and was granted a temporary deferment on the grounds of family hardship. Though he made inquiries about joining Ford's Field Photographic Unit, which produced documentaries, propaganda, and intelligence reports for the War Department, Wayne never followed through beyond the initial queries. By 1944, his deferment had expired, and Wayne was eligible for the draft. Republic Pictures, fearful of losing their star attraction, intervened on his behalf, and the actor did not object. He was given another deferment on the vague grounds of "national interest."

Wayne did visit U.S. bases and hospitals in the South Pacific during a three-month tour in 1943 and 1944. He was almost always warmly welcomed by the brass and the new enlistees, but according to eyewitness and bestselling historian William Manchester, during an appearance in Hawaii, the cowboy-hatted actor was booed off the stage by wounded soldiers. (The incident inspired a scene in the 2011 superhero movie *Captain America: The First Avenger*.)

According to Wayne's third and final wife, Peruvian actress Pilar Pallete, his failure to enlist weighed heavily upon his conscience for the rest of his life.

After the war, the one-time liberal became Hollywood's most visible conservative, and his on-screen persona embodied American strength. Every year from 1949 to 1974, Wayne was among the top ten biggest box-office stars. Whether battling Indians, as in the Ford movies, or the Japanese, as in *The Sands of Iwo Jima* (1949), he never played a villain. The forward-marching man of action also never apologized, an act which his character in *She Wore a Yellow Ribbon* called "a sign of weakness."

During the Red Scare of the 1950s, Wayne was a vocal anticommunist and a member of the ultra-conservative John Birch Society (a group with which he eventually parted ways). Soviet dictator Joseph Stalin wanted Wayne killed, an order that was rescinded by Stalin's successor, cowboy-movie aficionado Nikita Khrushchev.

By 1960, Wayne was middle-aged and wearing a hairpiece. He knew that his years as a matinee idol were coming to an end, so he added "director" to his résumé, with his epic version of the Alamo story. As with most of

Wayne's movies, *The Alamo* was one-sided, and its historical accuracy is dubious. But it was positively diplomatic compared to his second, and last, directorial effort, 1968's *The Green Berets*. Made in the midst of the anti-war protests that painted Wayne as a racist hypocrite, *The Green Berets* fought back, asserting that the Vietnam War was a just cause. It was the only studio movie that supported the war effort. Many reviewers ridiculed the film, but Wayne's loyal fans and the silent majority of moviegoers ensured that *The Green Berets* broke even. A year later, Wayne's peers awarded him his only Oscar, for his role as a drunken vigilante in *True Grit*.

In 1971, Wayne gave a controversial interview to *Playboy* magazine in which he affirmed his belief in "white supremacy" and opined that modern Native Americans and African Americans were owed no favors for past injustices.

Wayne, who smoked as many as six packs of cigarettes a day and made the Genghis Khan movie *The Conqueror* downwind from a Nevada nuclear test site, died of cancer in 1979. His towering presence still looms over the western territories. His name is affixed to a highway in Arizona, a marina in Washington State, and the main airport in Orange County, California. In front of the former Great Western bank building in Beverly Hills (now the headquarters of *Hustler* magazine), there is a bronze statue of Wayne astride a horse. The gun-toting figure is larger than life, just like a war hero. ★

John Wayne, an emblem of American bravado on screen, never served in the military. *Hulton Archive/ Stringer/Getty Images*

HUMPHREY BOGART

Was Bogie a Bolshevik?

*I*n his most famous role, Humphrey Bogart declared "I stick my neck out for nobody." In real life, when he stuck his neck out for his principles, it almost got chopped.

It's no myth that Bogart came into the world on Christmas Day, 1899. (For many years this was thought to have been a fictional birth date created by the Warner Bros. studio.) Hardly born in a manger, little Humphrey was the son of a Manhattan heart surgeon and a successful commercial illustrator. It's not true, as has been reported, that baby Bogart was the model for the infant on the Gerber baby foods label. Actually, his mother used drawings of her son in advertisements for a company called Mellin's Baby Food, which pre-dated the Gerber label by thirty years.

Bogart attended the exclusive Phillips Andover prep school in Massachusetts but was expelled for misbehavior. So he joined the Navy, just as World War I was ending. (Some accounts say Bogart injured his lip and acquired his trademark lisp when he was hit by shrapnel in a naval battle. Others say he was struck by a prisoner he was transporting. Still others say he was belted by his father during an argument.)

After the war, Bogart found a job as a stage manager in New York. Soon he transitioned to acting. Between 1922 and 1935, he appeared in at least seventeen Broadway productions, often playing an effete sort of character that Bogart later dubbed "White Pants Willie." During these years he

"Bogie," whose many influential roles included Sam Spade, Philip Marlowe, and Rick Blaine, was ranked as the greatest American male screen legend by the American Film Institute in 1999.
Pictorial Parade/ Getty Images

married twice, to actress Helen Menken in 1926 and to another actress, Mary Philips, in 1928, a year after his divorce from Menken.

When the stock market crash of 1929 curtailed stage production, Bogart signed a contract with the Fox Film Corporation in Hollywood. One of his first film roles was in his friend Spencer Tracy's first movie, a 1930 escaped-convict comedy called *Up the River*, directed by John Ford. Bogart spent the early 1930s shuttling back and forth between Hollywood and Broadway.

"Democrat in politics, Episcopalian by upbringing, dissenter by disposition."

— Humphrey Bogart

Bogart's life and image changed forever in 1935, the year he appeared as the villain in a Broadway drama called *The Petrified Forest*. The actor played a killer who terrorizes the patrons of a roadside restaurant, including one played by star Leslie Howard. When Warner Bros. bought the film rights for Howard, he said he wouldn't make the movie unless they also cast the little-known Bogart.

The success of the movie version of *The Petrified Forest* allowed Bogart to make a deal with Warner Bros., which then specialized in hard-boiled crime dramas. Although Bogart made more than twenty films between 1936 and 1940, it was not a happy time for him. He and Philips, who was still a bigger star than her husband, divorced in 1937, and in 1938 Bogart married yet another volatile actress, the hard-drinking Mayo Methot. At home, he fought with his wife; at the studio, he fought the executives who gave the best scripts to established stars like Edward G. Robinson, James Cagney, George Raft, and Paul Muni.

When the latter two actors turned down the lead in a gangster flick called *High Sierra* (1941), Bogart got a rare shot at an A-level script (written by his drinking buddy, John Huston). Raft also turned down Huston's directorial debut, *The Maltese Falcon* (also 1941), allowing Bogart to give what he considered his best performance yet. Soon after that film won the Academy Award for Best Picture of 1942, Bogart became the highest-paid actor in the world.

Despite his new wealth, the lifelong Democrat never lost his sympathy for the oppressed common man. When studio bosses, led by anti-unionist Walt Disney, started to sniff out suspected Communists in the film industry, Bogart became one of Hollywood's most vocal defenders of freedom of speech and assembly. In 1947, eleven screenwriters were subpoenaed to testify in Washington before the House of Un-American Activities Committee. Before the war, the same panel had heard vague accusations against actors including Bogart and Cagney, and by 1947, the Red Scare had heated up. Although it was not illegal to join the Communist Party, which had attracted as many as 50,000 Americans while the Soviets were U.S. allies against the Nazis, congressmen (including a young Richard Nixon) demanded to know if the writers were now or had ever been members of the party.

Bogart, John Huston, Danny Kaye, Gene Kelly, Henry Fonda, and Bogart's new wife, Lauren Bacall, lent support to the writers through a group called the Committee for the First Amendment. With Bogart in attendance at the hearing, ten of the writers refused to answer questions and were charged with contempt of Congress. (The eleventh writer, German émigré Bertolt Brecht, testified and promptly left the country.) The next day, the so-called Hollywood Ten were officially blacklisted by the studios. After the writers' appeals were turned down by the Supreme Court, all ten were sent to prison on the contempt charges.

Pressured by his bosses, Bogart wrote a 1948 article for *Photoplay* magazine titled "I'm No Communist." Although he did not disavow his friends or their rights, he wrote that some people in the industry had been "duped" by a small number of Communists and that he himself felt foolish for being linked with a party to which he would never belong.

The circle of suspicion continued to widen. In 1950, an FBI-funded magazine called *Counterattack* published a pamphlet titled *Red Channels* that listed 151 suspected Communists in the entertainment industry. The list included actors Edward G. Robinson, John Garfield, Burgess Meredith, and Zero Mostel; writers Arthur Miller, Dashiell Hammett, and Dorothy Parker; director Orson Welles; and even stripper Gypsy Rose Lee. Two years later, director Elia Kazan and writer Budd Schulberg testified to the committee against some former friends, an act that remains one of the most notorious in Hollywood history. (When Kazan was awarded an honorary Oscar in 1999, many audience members refused to applaud.)

Though Bogart drifted away from the studio system after his brush with the blacklist, the last decade of his life was his happiest. He satisfied himself with the pleasurable company of the much-younger Bacall and the professional company of trusted friends like Huston, who directed Bogart to his lone Oscar, for his role as a reluctant hero in 1951's *The African Queen*.

When asked what he believed in, Bogart would say baseball. "You yell like crazy for your guys," he said, "and nobody calls the cops." ★

MONTGOMERY CLIFT

Did a car crash turn the talented actor into a living wreck?

Officially, Montgomery Clift died in 1966 of heart failure. But it was a death ten years in the making. The onset was a car accident that demolished the only acting career that could have competed with Marlon Brando's.

Even Brando, who sneered at disciples such as James Dean, was intimidated by Clift. Clift was four years older than Brando and they were born in the same city: Omaha, Nebraska. Whereas Brando was a miserable, abused boy, young Clift was treated like a prince by a mother who was convinced that she was herself royalty. Ethel "Sunny" Clift was the illegitimate daughter of southern aristocrats who put her up for adoption. As an adult, she fought for her birth family's acceptance, and she groomed her handsome son (who also had a twin sister) to take his place in high society. Instead he found a place in the theater.

Clift made his Broadway debut at age fifteen in *Fly Away Home* (1935). Exempted from the draft because of an intestinal condition, he appeared in about a dozen major plays over the next decade, including works by Tennessee Williams and Thornton Wilder. Hollywood recruited him in 1946 to play the son of a cattle rancher (John Wayne) in *Red River*. The role required the androgynous newcomer to duke it out with the strapping embodiment of American manhood. Of Clift's performance, a *New York Times* reviewer wrote, "[He] has our admiration as the lean and leathery kid...and he carries it off splendidly."

"Monty" Clift at the height of his career in 1950. *From Here to Eternity* co-star Donna Reed remarked, "I had never worked with any actor like him. To watch him was incredible and memorable." *Getty Images*

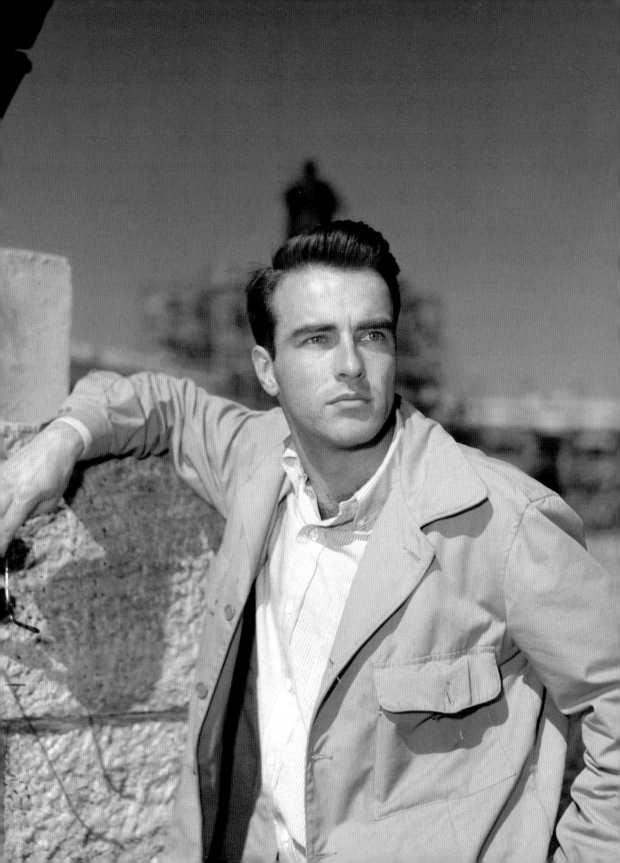

It was the first of several roles in which Clift's characters took a beating, but both on and off the screen, he never backed down. For his second film, a drama about concentration camp survivors called *The Search*, he essentially rewrote the script. His performance and the screenplay for which he wasn't credited were both nominated for Academy Awards.

Montgomery "Monty" Clift was a new breed of leading man, a sensitive loner whose wounded eyes told the story that his minimal words could not. Three times in six years, Clift was an Oscar nominee for Best Actor. From his perch in New York, he rejected countless scripts, including *Sunset Boulevard*, which had been written specifically for him, and the Western *Shane*. When Clift did assent to a movie, his co-stars felt the challenge to rise to his level. On the set of *From Here to Eternity* (1953), he effectively gave acting lessons to co-stars Donna Reed, Burt Lancaster, and Frank Sinatra. (Sinatra would go on to win an Oscar for his performance, as Best Supporting Actor.)

Clift's most famous student—and his loyal friend—was Elizabeth Taylor. They met on a blind date in 1949, when Paramount had Clift escort Taylor to the premiere of his film *The Heiress*. She was more than ten years his junior, a glamorous teen who would rather get married and have children than commit to serious acting, but their connection was immediate. Gossip columnists hinted at a romance, and Taylor did indeed want to marry Clift. Monty was extremely secretive about his relationships and was believed to prefer men, yet onscreen in *A Place in the Sun* (1951), there was a genuine erotic chemistry between the two beautiful stars.

On May 12, 1956, Taylor invited Clift to a dinner party at her Benedict Canyon home, where she had been feuding with her second husband, British actor Michael Wilding. Clift, who was filming the 1957 antebellum romance *Raintree County* with Taylor, wanted a rare day apart from the needy woman he called Bessie Mae, but Taylor insisted that he attend. Other guests included closeted actor Rock Hudson, Taylor's co-star in *Giant*; Hudson's wife-of-convenience Phyllis Gates; and Clift's actor friend Kevin McCarthy.

Because Wilding was in a jealous mood, the party was a bust. Clift decided to leave early. It was foggy on Mulholland Drive, and Clift was driving a car he rarely used, so McCarthy offered to lead the way, in his own car, down the hill.

On a hairpin turn, Clift lost control of his car and smashed into a utility pole. McCarthy rushed back to the house. Instead of calling an ambulance, Taylor ran to the scene, where she found Clift crumpled beneath the dashboard, his jaw broken and his nose practically ripped from his face. He signaled to Taylor that he couldn't breathe. Two of his teeth were lodged in his throat, and Taylor yanked them out, saving his life.

But his career could not be saved, and the disfigured star embarked on what has been called Hollywood's longest suicide. After reconstructive surgery on his face, he finished *Raintree County*. Although director Edward Dmytryk was careful to only film the right side of Clift's face, the before-and-after scenes were an awkward match.

After the film wrapped, Clift went into seclusion, with actor Jack Larson (Jimmy Olsen of the TV series *The Adventures of Superman*) as his help-mate. One day they were visited by Marlon Brando, who urged Clift to continue acting, if only to spur Brando to greatness.

Clift returned to the screen with Brando and Dean Martin in the 1958 war drama *The Young Lions*, a film that Clift considered his best. But pain-killers and alcohol took their toll. Taylor got him a role in *Suddenly, Last Summer* (1959), during which the director and producer were so unsympa-thetic to the addled actor that co-star Katharine Hepburn spat at them the minute the picture was finished.

On the set of *The Misfits* (1961), Clift found a kindred spirit in Marilyn Monroe, who described him as "the only person I know who is in worse shape than I am."

Clift, in constant pain, was so heavily medicated on the set of 1961's *Judgment at Nuremberg* that he could not remember his lines. Spencer Tracy, playing the tribunal judge to whom Clift's Holocaust survivor tes-tifies, pulled Clift aside and urged him to ignore the script and instead interact naturally with him. For the seven-minute scene, Clift earned his fourth and final Oscar nomination, this time in the supporting category.

While starring in the biopic *Freud* (1962), Clift was so argumentative with director John Huston that the studio sued the actor to recoup the cost of production delays. Clift didn't work for another four years. He became a ghostly figure on the fringe of Manhattan culture, attending matinee mov-ies in empty theaters and occasionally standing in the shadows at Andy Warhol's parties.

Taylor continued to worship Clift, and in 1965 she proposed that they star together in the love triangle *Reflections in a Golden Eye*, with fifth husband Richard Burton co-starring and directing. When Burton changed his mind about playing a subordinate role to the man who was his wife's real love, Huston agreed to direct if the production could be insured. Taylor offered to pay for the insurance, but there were no takers.

On July 23, 1966, *The Misfits* aired on New York television. Clift's live-in secretary asked him if he would like to watch it with him. "Absolutely not!" Clift exclaimed. Those would be his last words. He died that night at age forty-six, alone in his upstairs bedroom. ★

8

MARLON BRANDO

Did the method actor father a fiendish killer?

"That's not true!" shouted a voice at the back of the lecture hall. "My father is the greatest actor in the world!"

The voice belonged to Christian Brando, disrupting our Introduction to Film class at the University of Southern California in 1982. The guest lecturer that day was a screenwriter/producer named Steve Shagan, who was in the midst of describing how the student's father, Marlon Brando, had ruined a recent movie called *The Formula*.

The elder Brando had been paid almost $3 million for eleven days of work on the thriller, in which he played the devious chairman of an oil company. The actor refused to memorize his lines. Instead of relying on cue cards posted around the set, as he had been doing since *On The Waterfront* in 1954 (and which he took to such an extreme for 1972's *Last Tango in Paris* that he wanted to write his lines on co-star Maria Schneider's naked body), Brando wore an earpiece that resembled a hearing aid. The movie, based on Shagan's bestselling novel, was a flop. Brando was nominated for a Razzie Award for Worst Supporting Actor and retired from acting for the next decade. But in the classroom outburst, Christian was right. His father *was* the best actor in the world. And he would give one of his greatest performances when his son needed him most.

The Godfather, 1972.
© Pictorial Press Ltd/Alamy

Marlon Brando as Sky Masterson in *Guys and Dolls* (1955). Co-star Frank Sinatra, who wanted the role that Brando won, was said to have dismissively called Brando "Mumbles" on set. © *MARKA/Alamy*

Marlon Brando was born in Omaha, Nebraska, in 1924 to two alcoholic parents, a salesman father and an amateur-actress mother who had once mentored a local boy named Henry Fonda. After troubled young Marlon was kicked out of military school, he followed his actress sister Jocelyn to New York. There, Brando studied with acting instructor Stella Adler. Their collaboration would revolutionize both theatrical and film performance in the twentieth century. Adler taught "the Method," an approach to acting that tapped into the performer's personal memories.

Between 1944 and 1950, Brando acted in about a dozen Broadway productions. (For much of that time he lived with actor Wally Cox, who would later star in TV's *Mr. Peepers* and *Hollywood Squares*.) Brando's stage career culminated in his astonishing performance as a New Orleans roughneck in the 1947 play *A Streetcar Named Desire* by Tennessee Williams. Generations of actors have since attempted to ape Brando's mumbling delivery and forceful physicality, but his style has proved impossible to replicate.

When Brando traded Broadway for Hollywood, movies as diverse as the coming-home drama *The Men* (1950), the Shakespearean history *Julius Caesar* (1953), and the musical *Guys and Dolls* (1955) reflected a range of both professional talents and personal interests that bordered on eccentricity.

Brando replaced Stanley Kubrick in the director's chair for the Western *One-Eyed Jacks* in 1961, then repeated his takeover tactics the following year on the set of *Mutiny on the Bounty*. Although he was not officially the director of the big-budget remake, he was blamed for its ballooning budget and subsequent box-office failure.

In the 1960s, Brando diverted much of his attention to minority rights, at the expense of his career and family. Between 1957 and 1962, he married three times. He also fathered five legitimate children and an unknown number of illegitimate ones.

After Brando made a career comeback in *The Godfather* in 1972 (for which he sent a Native American actress named Sacheen Littlefeather onstage to refuse his Oscar), two of his oft-neglected children became particularly close. Christian (whose mother was Indian actress Anna Kashfi) was eleven years older than his sister Cheyenne (daughter of Tahitian actress Tarita Teriipia). As they shuttled back and forth between his father's home in Hollywood and private island in Tahiti, Christian grew protective of his little sister.

Cheyenne was a beauty, but she was prone to violent tantrums that suggested mental illness. On one occasion, when her father denied her request to join him on the Toronto set of *The Freshman* (1990), she grabbed the keys to her boyfriend's Jeep, sped away, and crashed. She was seriously scarred in the accident. Her boyfriend, Dag Drollet, became worried about her erratic behavior, which only increased when, after the accident, she became pregnant.

In May 1990, Christian arrived from Tahiti to visit Cheyenne and their father at his estate on Mulholland Drive. On May 16, he was introduced to Drollet, who declined the siblings' offer to join them for dinner. Over drinks at the historic Musso & Frank Grill on Hollywood Boulevard, Cheyenne, who was by then eight months pregnant, told Christian that Drollet was chronically violent toward her. It wasn't true, but Christian believed her.

When they returned to the house, Christian pulled out one of his many guns and shot Drollet. Christian's horror-stricken father, who was in another part of the house, rushed to help Drollet, who was the son of an old friend, but it was too late.

Christian was arrested and Cheyenne fled to Tahiti, where she gave birth to a boy and was diagnosed as schizophrenic. Because the prosecution's chief witness could not be extradited, the charge against Christian was reduced from first-degree murder to manslaughter.

At age sixty-six, the elder Brando stirred from his late-life torpor to coordinate the defense. He hired private investigators, ballistics experts, and pathologists, and he pledged his house as collateral for Christian's bail. The elder Brando was the star attraction at the pre-trial hearing, where he testified for several hours. He shouted, cried, apologized to the Drollet family in French, and confessed, "I led a wasted life. I chased a lot of women. Perhaps I failed as a father."

Christian pled guilty. The judge declared that the shooting had been a tragedy for both families and sentenced the son to a relatively lenient ten years in prison. He was released after five. While Christian was in prison, twenty-five-year-old Cheyenne hung herself at her mother's home in Tahiti.

After his stint in prison, Christian moved to Washington State, where he worked as a welder and tree trimmer. He also dated a groupie named Bonnie Lee Bakley, who gave birth to a girl named Christian Shannon Brando. When DNA tests proved that the baby was actually the child of Brando-esque ex-TV star Robert Blake, Christian was recorded telling Bakley that she deserved to be shot.

She was, by an unknown assailant, after dining with Blake on May 4, 2001. Blake was acquitted of the murder four years later, and Bakley's death remains an unsolved mystery.

Marlon Brando died of natural causes on July 1, 2001. Christian died seven years later, of pneumonia. ★

9

JERRY LEWIS

Did the nutty professor concoct and discard a masterpiece?

$\mathcal{M}$ost of the movies in Hollywood history are lost forever. Countless silent films deteriorated or were discarded to make room in the studio vaults. Other movies were mangled by producers who didn't respect the directors' wishes. Among the legendary films considered lost are Alfred Hitchcock's silent *The Mountain Eagle* (1927) and Ernst Lubitch's *The Patriot* (an Oscar nominee for Best Picture in 1928), as well as the director's cuts of Erich Von Stroheim's *Greed* (1924) and Orson Welles' *The Magnificent Ambersons* (1942). In 1987, Woody Allen shot a version of his marital drama *September*, shelved the completed film, then replaced the cast for a do-over.

Few lost films are as mythic as Jerry Lewis' 1972 Holocaust drama *The Day the Clown Cried*. Some connoisseurs of kitsch have speculated that the sight of the comedian doing his trademark shtick in a concentration camp was so horrific that the movie was mothballed. Others have suggested that the subject matter was so unnerving for Lewis that he insisted that the film not be released until after his death. The reality is that the movie is trapped in a typical Hollywood standoff between Lewis, the screenwriters, and the investors.

Lewis was born Joseph Levitch in Newark, New Jersey, in 1926. He honed his brand of broad humor at the Borscht Belt variety clubs in the Catskill Mountains in New York, where his trademark was a skit in which he mimed the lyrics to an operatic record that was playing off stage.

In July 1946, Lewis had a gig at the 500 Club in Atlantic City. When the club needed a last-minute replacement for a canceled act, the nineteen-year-old comedian suggested a crooner he had met a year earlier, a handsome Italian-American who called himself Dean Martin (real name: Dino Crocetti, from Steubenville, Ohio). On short notice, the two men concocted an act that consisted of the comedian interrupting and insulting the singer. They were an immediate hit. Soon Martin and Lewis had their own radio show and a ticket to Hollywood.

Between 1950 and 1956, Martin and Lewis were the top box-office attraction in the world. They stuck to a fail-safe formula: Dean was the ladies' man forced to babysit spastic man-child Jerry. After an acrimonious breakup during which Martin told his partner "You're nothing to me but a [bleeping] paycheck," Lewis went solo. He was on an annual list of top-ten Hollywood money-makers for six out of the next eight years.

The two men switched roles. Martin became a comic figure, the designated drunkard in Frank Sinatra's Rat Pack, and Lewis redefined himself as an artiste, writing and directing his own movies while teaching film at the University of Southern California.

Lewis' proudest professional achievement was *The Nutty Professor*, a 1963 Jekyll-and-Hyde comedy about a clumsy chemist who morphs into a lascivious lounge singer. French intellectuals—some of whom hailed the actor as the next Charlie Chaplin or Buster Keaton—debated whether the arrogant Buddy Love character was a doppelgänger for Dean Martin, or possibly a reflection of Lewis' own dark side.

The duality in Lewis' character seems to have spun out of control on *The Day the Clown Cried*. The script, about a German circus performer who insults Adolf Hitler and is sent to a concentration camp, was written by Joan O'Brien, a publicist who had worked with circus legend Emmett Kelly, and Charles Denton, a newspaper columnist and television critic. During the 1960s, the lead role attracted the attention of performers ranging from comedian Milton Berle to singer Bobby Darin. In 1971, producer Nat Wachsberger had an option on the script and pitched it to Lewis. To his credit, Lewis thought he couldn't carry a dramatic role. To his discredit, he agreed to do the film if he could direct it and rewrite the script.

In Lewis' version, the gentile clown, Helmut Doork (a name created by Lewis), does an unflattering imitation of Hitler and is sent to a concentration camp, where he meets Jewish children bound for the death camp at Auschwitz. Because his buffoonery makes the children laugh, the commandant decides that Doork is a handy tool to keep things calm on the train.

Lewis deliberately lost thirty pounds on a grapefruit diet, then worked feverishly hard on the film, which was shot in Sweden in 1972. At the time he was battling both an addiction to the painkiller Percodan and his own demons.

When Wachsberger fled to the French Riviera shortly after production began, the sleep-deprived Lewis contributed his own money to the project, only to discover that the producer's option on the script had already expired. The screenwriters sued to halt production after filming was complete but before editing had begun. The Swedish courts intervened and seized the footage, but not before Lewis was able to save the last reel and a videotape of the completed film.

Among the few who have seen the rough cut of the movie is satirist Harry Shearer of *This is Spinal Tap* fame. In an article for *Spy* magazine, he discussed how Lewis' mix of misplaced sympathies and misdirected slapstick crossed the border of bad taste.

Shearer had found the film through an acquaintance who worked on Lewis' annual telethon for the Muscular Dystrophy Association. Like a lot of lot of pop-culture critics from the post-vaudeville generation, Shearer finds the telethon morbidly fascinating. Although it should never be forgotten that Lewis has helped raise more than $2 billion for neuromuscular research, his emotional arm-twisting and blunt remarks have rubbed some people—including disability rights advocates and the charity's own board of directors—the wrong way. In 2011, the MDA abruptly fired Lewis as chairman and telethon host.

Until the world can see and judge *The Day the Clown Cried* for itself, there will remain unresolved questions about Lewis' legacy. In Martin Scorsese's 1983 film *The King of Comedy*, Lewis was unnervingly good as a cynical, self-protective talk-show host. Perhaps he was equally good in *Clown*'s dramatic role, twenty-five years before Roberto Benigni won an Oscar for a similar role in *Life Is Beautiful*.

Unless reps for the director, producer, and writers free the hostage *Clown*, we may never know. ★

10

ELVIS PRESLEY

Did the King leave his crown at a Hollywood pawn shop?

He was the king of rock'n'roll (although certainly not its inventor). Yet in his prime, Elvis Presley spent more time and effort making movies than music.

Music came naturally to Presley, who had perfect pitch and was raised in the gospel tradition in Tupelo, Mississippi (where he was born in 1935), and Memphis, Tennessee. His meteoric rise to stardom, which started at age eighteen when he paid for a few minutes of studio time at Sun Records in Memphis to record a ballad for his mother's birthday, is as well documented as the life of a saint.

That meteor dimmed after 1958, when Presley was drafted into the Army. When he returned from Germany in 1960, his singles and soundtracks continued to sell, but he rarely performed in public until after a 1968 TV broadcast, now often referred to as the '68 *Comeback Special*. Presley spent the intervening years shuttling between his Memphis home, his Vegas playground, and his Hollywood workplace.

Before his tour of duty, he had made four movies that effectively showcased his natural charisma and the tricks he had gleaned from Marlon Brando while working as a movie usher in Memphis. In the Civil War potboiler *Love Me Tender* (1956), Presley played a supporting role (and sang four songs). In *Loving You* and *Jailhouse Rock*, both 1957, he essentially played himself. The following year, for the delinquency drama *Kid Creole*, respected

producer Hal Wallis teamed Presley with Michael Curtiz, the director of *Casablanca*, and established stars Walter Matthau and Carolyn Jones.

After Presley returned from the army, his profit-driven manager, Tom Parker, encouraged him to take a role in *G.I. Blues* (1960) instead of the now-classic movie version of *West Side Story*. Over the next nine years, Presley would make another twenty-six feature films. They all made money; none were art. Even Presley said that they were produced on an assembly line. But at least one of them had a magic chemistry. In *Viva Las Vegas* (1964), Presley was paired for the first and only time with a co-star who was his equal in talent and sex appeal: Ann-Margret. The two had a long affair.

Presley aspired to be as artistically and socially relevant as the Beatles (who visited their idol at his Bel Air mansion and offered in vain to make a cameo appearance in his movie *Paradise, Hawaiian Style*), but Parker prevented him from flipping the script. The manager nixed the idea of Presley co-starring with John Wayne in *True Grit* or Barbra Streisand in *A Star Is Born* because the studios wouldn't agree to give Presley top billing or a million-dollar salary. So instead, Presley did a few lesser Westerns along with countless race-car movies and romantic travelogues (all of which were filmed in the United States because Parker was an illegal Dutch immigrant who couldn't risk leaving the country). Reportedly Presley was intimate with every one of his comely co-stars except the last: Mary Tyler Moore in *A Change of Habit* (1969).

Presley never became a great actor; nor did he ever lose his love of movies. He often rented out entire Memphis theaters and drive-ins so he and his posse could watch the latest films undisturbed by fans. His favorites included *Rebel Without a Cause*, *Dr. Strangelove*, *Bullitt*, and *Dirty Harry*. In the last week of his life, he tried in vain to secure a print of a new sensation called *Star Wars* to show his daughter, Lisa Marie.

Elvis died in his Graceland bathroom on August 16, 1977, under mysterious circumstances that have inspired an entire library of myth-buster books. ★

Myths about Elvis abound and pertain to everything from his eating habits (yes, he really did love peanut butter, banana, and bacon sandwiches) to his afterlife (no, he's not still alive—probably). *Michael Ochs Archives/Getty Images*

11

WOODY ALLEN

Is the director guilty of crimes and misdemeanors?

Woody Allen did not marry his daughter, adopted or otherwise. Soon-Yi Previn, whom Allen married in 1997, is the adopted daughter of Mia Farrow and conductor André Previn. Farrow and Allen were an unmarried couple for a dozen years, during which Allen adopted two of her children and fathered another. But Soon-Yi wasn't one of them.

To some people that's nitpicking. Those people include Farrow, whose break-up and subsequent custody fight with Allen were very public and very bitter, with charges of molestation tossed into the mix. While Allen may be a cad, he's not a criminal.

Born Allen Stewart Konigsberg in Brooklyn in 1935, Woody Allen got his start in show business as a gag writer. After being expelled from New York University (for bad grades and not, as he quipped, for looking into the soul of the philosophy student sitting next to him), he became a standup comedian with a distinctively neurotic personality.

Warren Beatty signed him to write and co-star in the 1965 swinging sex comedy *What's New Pussycat?*, but Beatty quit when Allen gave himself all the best jokes. (Beatty was replaced by Peter O'Toole.) Soon Allen was writing and directing his own projects. After a string of "early, funny ones" that were heavily influenced by Bob Hope and the Marx Brothers, Allen matured into a serious filmmaker, adding existential angst to the Borscht

Woody Allen and Soon-Yi Previn have been married since 1997. In 2011, while promoting *Midnight in Paris*, Allen said, "There was no scandal, but people refer to it all the time as a scandal and I kind of like that…. When I go I would like to say I had one real juicy scandal in my life."
WireImage/Getty Images

Belt menu. He developed a reputation for eccentricity—for instance, on the night in 1978 when *Annie Hall* earned him Academy Awards for Best Picture, Best Director, and Best Original Screenplay, Allen was busy playing his weekly clarinet gig at Michael's Pub in New York City.

It was his black-and-white masterpiece *Manhattan* (1979) that started the whispers about his private life. In the film, Allen's forty-ish character has an affair with a high-school girl. The role, played by Mariel Hemingway, was reportedly based on Allen's off-screen tryst with a teenager named Stacey Nelkin, whose small role in *Annie Hall* had been left on the cutting-room floor. At the time, Allen had been in a long-term relationship with his frequent leading lady Diane Keaton. The same pattern would be repeated with Farrow.

Mia Farrow, the waifish daughter of Australian writer and director John Farrow (an Oscar winner for writing *Around the World in 80 Days*) and Irish actress Maureen O'Sullivan (who played Jane in the Johnny Weissmuller *Tarzan* movies) was thirty-five when she met Allen, but looked about fifteen. Farrow had already lived a dizzying life. The star of the prime-time soap opera *Peyton Place* was twenty-one when she married fifty-year-old crooner Frank Sinatra. The marriage lasted two years, during which Farrow starred in *Rosemary's Baby* and fled to India to sit at the feet of the Maharishi Mahesh Yogi with the Beatles. In 1970, Farrow married Oscar-winning composer Previn (*Gigi*), with whom she would later adopt eight-year-old Korean girl Soon-Yi.

Farrow would eventually adopt eleven children, many of them foreigners with special needs. (Angelina Jolie should send her a thank-you note. Farrow helped persuade Congress to change the laws limiting the number of foreign children individual Americans can adopt.) Farrow also had three biological children with Previn. The couple divorced in 1979, and the following year, she and Woody Allen were an item.

Allen directed Farrow in thirteen movies, including *Zelig* (1983), *The Purple Rose of Cairo* (1985), and *Hannah and Her Sisters* (1986). They lived in apartments on opposites sides of Central Park and would wave towels out the window to each other as they spoke on the phone. Eventually they had a son together named Satchel.

One day in 1992, while Farrow was visiting Allen, she found a stack of nude Polaroids he had taken of twenty-one-year-old Soon-Yi. He claimed they were test shots for her prospective modeling career.

It didn't take long for the story to go public. Rumors about Allen's peccadilloes and Farrow's angry reaction (she was said to have sent Allen a valentine with pictures of the family being pierced with meat skewers) spread through the media and became fail-safe fixtures in talk-show monologues.

Around the time that Allen held a press conference to announce that he loved Soon-Yi, Farrow filed papers to win full custody of their three children. In court, she claimed that their adopted seven-year-old daughter, Dylan, said she had been molested by Allen. Although Dylan's own psychiatrist cast doubt on the story and Allen was never charged, the court sided with Farrow in the custody case. Their biological child, Satchel, pronounced his father unforgivable and changed his name to Ronan. (A child prodigy, he graduated from Bard College at fifteen, entered Yale at seventeen, worked as a human-rights activist in the State Department, and became a Rhodes Scholar in 2011.)

For her part, Soon-Yi says she never regarded Allen as a father, stepfather, or authority figure. Their relationship has lasted far longer than the ones he had with Farrow and Keaton. The Allens now have two adopted daughters of their own.

Allen still manages to make about one film a year. In 2011, the romantic fantasy *Midnight in Paris* became the biggest hit of his career. ★

"To love is to suffer. To avoid suffering, one must not love. But, then one suffers from not loving. Therefore, to love is to suffer, not to love is to suffer, to suffer is to suffer."

— Boris Grushenko in Woody Allen's *Love and Death*, 1975

12

HARRISON FORD

Was Indiana Jones a sidekick to Wally Cleaver?

When I asked Harrison Ford if he had been a cast member on the 1950s sitcom *Leave it to Beaver*, the famously gruff actor looked at me as if I were from outer space. But I hadn't invented the rumor, and I wasn't the only one to wonder if it might be true.

Officially, the future Indiana Jones first appeared on screen in 1966, in an uncredited role as a bellboy in the caper *Dead Heat on a Merry-Go-Round*. The Chicago native was twenty-two years old. There are plenty of Ford sightings for the video bloodhound to sniff out from the late 1960s and early 1970s, including bit parts in the hippie-era films *Luv* (1967) and *Getting Straight* (1970). A larger role in the 1970 student-revolt flick *Zabriskie Point* was left on the cutting-room floor. Ford also appeared in the TV series *Gunsmoke*, *Kung-Fu*, *The Mod Squad*, and even the romantic anthology series *Love, American Style*. He gradually worked his way up the Francis Ford Coppola–George Lucas ladder with small roles in *American Graffiti* (1973), *The Conversation* (1974), and 1979's *Apocalypse Now* (he played a character named Colonel Lucas) before really making a name for himself in three *Star Wars* and four *Indiana Jones* movies. He earned an Oscar nomination for *Witness* in 1985.

In some of his early appearances, the actor was billed as "Harrison J. Ford," even though he doesn't actually have a middle name. The initial was included to distinguish him from a silent-screen star named Harrison

Harrison Ford in Indiana Jones and the Last Crusade, thirty years after he may or may not have played Wally Cleaver's school friend. Photograph by Murray Close. Moviepix/ Getty Images

Ford, as union rules prevent two actors from using the same moniker. The ambiguous identifier may have contributed to the rumor that Ford had been a child actor under a different name. The main evidence, however, was photographic.

From 1957 to 1960, there was a minor character on *Leave It to Beaver* named Chester Anderson, an adolescent classmate of Wally Cleaver. The credits identified the young actor as "Buddy Hart," yet movie buffs watching reruns in the 1980s noticed that the kid looked an awful lot like a young Han Solo. In the Internet era, the rumor that Ford had co-starred on *Leave It to Beaver* hit warp speed, culminating when, circa 2000, talk-show host David Letterman confronted Ford with the video evidence. After viewing a clip of Buddy Hart in the beloved sitcom about Eisenhower-era suburbia, Ford gave one of his bemused half smiles but feigned ignorance.

I couldn't shake the suspicion that Ford was hiding something under his rumpled fedora, so in 2002, when I interviewed him about the submarine thriller *K-19: The Widowmaker*, I waited until my last question to spring my *Beaver* trap. Even though the issue had been addressed by Letterman on national television, Ford pretended he didn't know what I was talking about.

So I did some digging, and the silly, circumstantial coincidences beckoned like a golden idol. Buddy Hart has no screen credits after 1968, the approximate year when the actor Harrison J. Ford first appeared. (Incidentally, Hart's last credit is for a submarine thriller.) Officially Hart was the son of cowboy actor John Hart, who substituted for star Clayton Moore in several episodes of the 1950s TV series *The Lone Ranger*. The Hart family, then, included a masked man who borrowed someone else's identity. And what did Harrison Ford play in the big-screen adaptation of *The Fugitive*? A man who lies about his real name.

Today Ford spends most of his time on a secluded Wyoming ranch with wife Calista Flockhart (formerly of television's *Ally McBeal*). As to Buddy Hart's whereabouts, they remain a mystery—he's never been found. Maybe he's in the warehouse at Area 51 where Spielberg keeps the Ark of the Covenant. ★

13

ARNOLD SCHWARZENEGGER

Did the Terminator earn his success fair and square?

*H*is story seems too good to be true: a muscle-bound immigrant with a funny name and a thick accent becomes the biggest movie star in the world, marries into America's most distinguished family, and becomes governor of California. But Arnold Schwarzenegger's story contains more than a few "true lies." It turns out that his muscles, his marriage, and his mandate to govern were all artificially enhanced.

The fairy tale begins in a small village in Austria, where Arnold was born in 1947. His father was a former Nazi soldier-turned-policeman who beat the boy, who he believed was not his biological son.

Arnold loved soccer, but when he discovered weightlifting around age fourteen, it changed his life. Determined to look like Hollywood bodybuilder Steve Reeves, Schwarzenegger fanatically trained both his body and mind.

At eighteen, he served a mandatory year in the Austrian army, but he went AWOL to compete in the Mr. Junior Europe bodybuilding competition. He won the competition—and then spent a week in military prison. In 1966 he traveled to London for the Mr. Universe competition, where he finished in second place. A coach was impressed with the strapping lad and invited him to move to England to train.

In London, Schwarzenegger honed his leg strength and rudimentary English. At age twenty, he became the youngest competitor to win the title

of Mr. Universe. He would win that title three more times. He won the more prestigious Mr. Olympia competition seven times, including in 1980, when he was already an established actor who had officially retired from bodybuilding.

Schwarzenegger's dedication to and legacy in bodybuilding cannot be questioned. But his ethics can. He has admitted that during his competitive career he used steroids to retain muscle mass on his frame (officially listed as six feet two inches but subject to debate). He estimated that the drugs gave him a five-percent edge on the other competitors. Over time, he has added that the drugs were prescribed by a doctor and were not as potent as the black-market steroids available today. Once he started running for political office, he changed his tune and repudiated steroids altogether. It is not known whether, like professional rival (and former Planet Hollywood partner) Sylvester Stallone, he used steroids to bulk up for movie roles.

Schwarzenegger's first film was 1970's *Hercules in New York*, for which he was billed as "Arnold Strong." Because of his thick accent, his dialogue had to be dubbed by another actor. For his role as a hit man in Robert Altman's *The Long Goodbye* (1973), Schwarzenegger did not have to talk—the part was changed to a deaf-mute. He used his own voice in the quasi-documentary *Stay Hungry* (1976) and leveraged his accent when he played Hungarian bodybuilder Mickey Hargitay in the television biopic *The Jayne Mansfield Story* in 1980. Perhaps the most ingenious—and profitable—use of his linguistic limitations was in the phenomenally successful *Terminator* series. He played a cyborg who could only utter catchphrases.

Schwarzenegger, already rich and recognizable from his bodybuilding career, had become wealthy and famous beyond his wildest dreams. In 1986, he added another trophy to his collection when he married television news personality Maria Shriver, the niece of slain U.S. president John F. Kennedy. Soon Schwarzenegger became a political player too. He was a fitness spokesman for President Ronald Reagan (while First Lady Nancy Reagan was urging kids to "Just say no" to drugs), and in his movies he was the artillery-toting, cigar-chomping embodiment of American might. He bought a Hummer military vehicle and made it street-legal, then convinced the company to sell the trucks to the general public.

Schwarzenegger's movie career started to wane in the 1990s, so he shifted his focus to politics. In 2003, California was suffering from the burst of the dot-com bubble and from an energy crisis exacerbated by the machinations at the Enron Corporation. Soon after colorless governor Gray Davis was reelected to a second term in office, conservative U.S. congressman Darrell Issa used $1.7 million of his own money to bankroll a recall petition and force Davis from office. Issa hoped to become governor himself. But in the midst of the petition drive, Schwarzenegger went on *The Tonight Show*

In 1980, while training to play the lead role in *Conan the Barbarian*, Schwarzenegger won his seventh Mr. Olympia title. *Hulton Archive/ Getty Images*

and announced his intention to replace Davis in the governor's chair. Issa begrudgingly endorsed him.

During the campaign, Schwarzenegger declined several opportunities to debate other contenders, hid his political opinions behind pun-filled catchphrases, and was outed as a serial groper of female acquaintances. Yet on October 7, 2003, Schwarzenegger won the most votes of the 135 candidates (including actor Gary Coleman), with 48.6 percent of the vote.

Governor Schwarzenegger inherited an intractable budget mess and steered a path that many pundits deemed centrist. He was handily reelected in 2006. After the financial collapse of 2008, his approval ratings sank to the lowest level ever recorded for a California governor: just 22 percent.

In 2011, as Schwarzenegger was leaving office and planning to resume his movie career—perhaps with a new version of *The Terminator*, an adaptation of the comic-book *The Governator*, or the border-town shoot-'em-up *The Last Stand*—it was revealed that he had fathered a child in 1997 with a former housekeeper (whom he had ensconced in a suburban home). Shriver, the loyal First Lady of California and mother of Schwarzenegger's other four children, announced that she was filing for divorce after twenty-five years of marriage. Schwarzenegger briefly went into seclusion, then declared that he would not be offering Shriver spousal support. Later he withdrew that defiant declaration and said he would set the record straight in his upcoming memoir.

In 2012, Schwarzenegger was in discussions to make a sequel to 1988's *Twins* with Danny DeVito and another dimmed star, Eddie Murphy. As of this writing, it's hard to predict whether the next catchphrase Schwarzenegger utters will be "I'll be back" or "Hasta la vista, baby." ★

EDDIE MURPHY

Did the golden child lose his Midas touch?

*L*ike the character Eddie Murphy played in *The Nutty Professor* (1996), Murphy's movies have been both playful and poisonous. Few actors have experienced such a wild ride on the wheel of fortune. Murphy went from comic phenomenon to action hero to family-film chameleon to box-office jinx of cosmic proportions. On the night when he expected to be crowned the comeback king, he was royally humiliated.

Murphy owned the 1980s. The Brooklyn-born stand-up comic started the decade as a nineteen-year-old cast member on *Saturday Night Live*. With his versions of Gumby, Buckwheat, and Mr. Rogers, he was a breakout star who revived the show in the post-John-Belushi era. In 1982, playing a motor-mouthed sidekick, Murphy stole the cop comedy *48 Hours* from its ostensible star, Nick Nolte. When Nolte fell ill before a scheduled *SNL* hosting gig, Murphy stole that too, becoming the first cast member to host the show.

He played other streetwise characters in the hits *Trading Places* (1983) and *Beverly Hills Cop* (1984) and starred in the profanity-ridden documentaries *Eddie Murphy Delirious* (1983) and *Eddie Murphy Raw* (1987). Surprisingly, Murphy's boyhood idol was Elvis Presley, and in the late 1980s, Murphy recorded some harmless party songs that would have damaged the street cred of a less-confident performer. On camera, Murphy was almost always smiling, but it was a dangerous smile that he could use to outwit those who underestimated him.

Eventually Murphy's smile froze into a permanent, goofy grin, and the father of at least eight children (with at least four different women) found a niche in family films. Taking a page from another of his idols, Peter Sellers, Murphy played multiple roles in a wholesome version of *The Nutty Professor*, a remake of the 1963 Jerry Lewis comedy. That hit movie has set the bar for his aspirations since 1996.

While comedies such as 1998's *Dr. Doolittle* and 2003's *Daddy Day Care* were lucrative, they limited Murphy's options and damaged his reputation. So did his 1997 arrest. Cops stopped Murphy as he was driving on Santa Monica Boulevard in West Hollywood at 4 a.m., accompanied by a transvestite prostitute named Shalomar. The star alleged that he was just giving a needy stranger a ride and some spending money. The police determined that nothing illegal had taken place, and they gave Murphy a simple warning in exchange for his autograph. (Shalomar was not so lucky. She was arrested on an outstanding warrant and died a year later in a mysterious fall from her apartment-building roof.)

Another low point in his life was the 2002 release of *The Adventures of Pluto Nash*. A sci-fi comedy about a retired smuggler who operates a nightclub on the moon in the year 2080, the film cost over $100 million to produce—and earned about $4 million at the U.S. box office. Some analysts consider it the costliest flop in the history of Hollywood. It wasn't Murphy's only fiasco. References to *Holy Man* (1998) and *Meet Dave* (2008) still evoke shudders from studio executives.

In 2006, he got a chance for redemption in *Dreamgirls*, the movie musical loosely based on the career of The Supremes. Murphy gave a powerful performance in the role of the girls' manager and was nominated for an Academy Award as Best Supporting Actor. In the weeks before the ceremony, he was touted as the favorite to win—until, that is, *Norbit*, another crass Eddie Murphy comedy, came out just before voting ended. On the night of the Oscars, Murphy lost the award to Alan Arkin for *Little Miss Sunshine*. Murphy quickly left the auditorium in a huff.

If you count the three *Shrek* movies, for which Murphy provides the voice of Donkey, Eddie Murphy is the number-two box-office star of all time, behind Tom Hanks.

In 2011, Murphy reverted to his streetwise persona in the middling hit *Tower Heist* and was named the host of the 2012 Academy Awards. But just a few months after securing the huge comeback gig, Murphy quit as Oscar host to show support for fired telecast producer Brett Ratner, who had angered the Academy with a homophobic wisecrack on Howard Stern's radio show.

Despite the subsequent release of the long-shelved comedy *A Thousand Words*, Murphy calls himself a semi-retired gentleman of leisure. Theater owners and the Academy of Motion Picture Arts and Sciences call him something else. ★

Eddie Murphy was ranked the most overpaid actor by *Forbes* magazine in 2011. *Time & Life Pictures/Getty Images*

15

TOM CRUISE

Is the megastar miniscule and mind-controlled?

Tom Cruise with Nicole Kidman in 1992. The couple made three films together (*Days of Thunder*, *Far and Away*, and *Eyes Wide Shut*) and adopted two children. *Photograph by Ron Galella. WireImage/Getty Images*

You've heard the hateful rumors, but compared to other movie stars, Tom Cruise is neither particularly short nor all that strange. When he flashes that famous smile, Cruise makes a positive impression. I met him in 2002, during a round-table interview for his movie *Minority Report*. When Cruise entered the room, he thoughtfully circled around the table, shaking hands with each of the half-dozen reporters. That's rare, so I made a point of standing up. I immediately noticed two things: The box-office superstar was wearing clear braces on his teeth, and (factoring in the boot heel that peeked out from the hem of his designer jeans) he was about 5 feet 7 inches—two inches less than average for an American man, but hardly short. And he's taller than a lot of famous actors who aren't taunted for their height. Tough-guy Jimmy Cagney was comparatively a shrimp at 5 feet 4 inches. Dustin Hoffman was 5 feet 5 inches when he made *The Graduate*. *Harry Potter* star Daniel Radcliffe is listed as 5 feet 6 inches, but in person, he is shorter than his similarly listed co-star Emma Watson. Alan Ladd, at 5 feet 6 inches, had to stand on an apple crate for some of his love scenes. Humphrey Bogart was 5 feet 8 inches and wearing two-inch lifts when he told his 5 feet 10 inches *Casablanca* co-star, "Here's looking at you, kid."

So why the special scorn reserved for Cruise? Part of it might be pity for Nicole Kidman, who stands 5 feet 11 inches but shrank into Cruise's

shadow during the ten-year marriage that she still won't talk about. But surely part of the hostility against Cruise is a mix of aversion to his religious beliefs and a peculiar desire to wipe the grin off the face of a seemingly too-happy person.

Thomas Cruise Mapother IV was born in upstate New York in 1962. His engineer father, whom Cruise has described as a coward and a bully, moved the family to Canada, Kentucky, Missouri, and New Jersey before leaving them when Cruise was eleven. As a teenager, Cruise briefly attended a Catholic seminary in Cincinnati, where he studied for the priesthood before turning his attention to high school musicals.

After graduation, Cruise gave himself a ten-year deadline to become famous (a deadline that swiftly proved unnecessary). He was a tireless auditioner in New York and then Los Angeles, where he landed an agent and small roles in *Endless Love* (1981), *Taps* (1981), Francis Ford Coppola's *The Outsiders* (1983), and the sex comedy *Losin' It* (1983). His first starring role, as a high-school overachiever who runs an escort service in *Risky Business* (1983), put his smile to good use. For much of the 1980s Cruise coasted through roles as a young hotshot who is humanized by a good woman. If 1986's *Top Gun* was the zenith of Reagan-era cockiness, *Cocktail* (1988) was its nadir. Cruise added shadings to his trademark persona in *The Color of Money* (1986) and *Rain Man* (1988). He earned an Oscar nomination for his performance as a disabled vet in Oliver Stone's *Born on the Fourth of July* (1989).

In 1987, Cruise married Mimi Rogers, an actress six years his senior, who introduced him to the Church of Scientology. The marriage lasted three years, but Cruise's relationship with the religion has only intensified. He credits Scientology with helping him overcome dyslexia and focus on his career. It also helped him woo Kidman, the Hawaii-born, Australia-raised beauty who was his co-star in the 1990 race-car movie *Days of Thunder*. When Cruise mentioned to a church official that he fantasized about running with Kidman through a field of wildflowers, volunteers worked night and day to plant a field for them.

For the first of the *Mission: Impossible* movies, Cruise earned $75 million by forgoing an upfront payday to take a hefty percentage of the gross. By the start of the new millennium he was arguably the biggest star in the world.

But then, in 2001, he divorced Kidman, with whom he has two adopted children, purportedly because she wanted to raise their children Catholic. Kidman was three months pregnant at the time. (She later miscarried.)

Cruise's image took another hit when he publicly criticized actress Brooke Shields for using prescribed drugs to cope with postpartum depression. Cruise explained in a contentious interview with Matt Lauer on *The Today Show* that Scientology does not believe in the pharmaceutical treatment of emotional conditions. That interview renewed debates about the tenets of Scientology, whose founder, L. Ron Hubbard, wrote that unhappy people were haunted by ghosts from a long-ago catastrophe.

When Cruise bounced atop Oprah Winfrey's couch while proclaiming his love for actress Katie Holmes (who is 5 feet 9 inches), cynics claimed that he was being forced into a sham marriage because someone had a damning dossier on him. Some haters also suggested that numerous reports about Cruise being a good Samaritan toward injured motorists, mugging victims, and trampled fans were exaggerated for publicity purposes.

Soon after the couch incident, Paramount ended its fourteen-year relationship with Cruise, citing the actor's controversial behavior as the reason. However, some analysts suggested that this was really just a studio ploy to renegotiate Cruise's share of DVD sales. Cruise has been a shrewd player in the new Hollywood that relies less on the American box office than on foreign sales and home video. In 2011, his globe-trotting action sequel *Mission Impossible: Ghost Protocol* earned good reviews and almost $700 million, two-thirds of it overseas. Cruise is a seriously savvy actor and businessman who understands that no matter what journalists and gossips say about his religion, his sex life, or his height, he'll always be big in Japan. ★

"I disagree with people who think you learn more from getting beat up than you do from winning."

— Tom Cruise

PART 2

Odd
COUPLES

16

FRED ASTAIRE AND GINGER ROGERS

Was it cheek to cheek—or just check to check?

Many have heard of the casting agent's curt dismissal of Fred Astaire: "Can't sing. Can't act. Balding. Can dance a little." But nobody has read the memo—because it doesn't seem to exist. Another myth about Astaire is that he and Ginger Rogers were an off-screen couple. Unlike Tracey and Hepburn or Bogart and Bacall, the dancing duo of Astaire and Rogers kept it strictly professional. By most accounts, Fred Astaire was a church-going conservative who genuinely loved his wife, Phyllis Potter, who died in 1954. But when the cameras were rolling it was a different story—in their ten films together, Fred and Ginger were the personification of romantic chemistry.

Frederick Austerlitz was born in 1899 in Omaha, Nebraska. When his father lost his brewery job, the family moved to New York so young Fred and his talented sister Adele could try to make it in show business. Renamed the Astaires, the nimble-footed siblings were a hit on the vaudeville circuit. In 1916, Fred met an aspiring songwriter named George Gershwin, who provided the dancers with fresh material that they showcased on both sides of the Atlantic.

The brother-sister act broke up in 1932, when Adele married a British lord. But with new partners, Fred continued to prosper on Broadway, and Hollywood movie studios were soon courting him.

While it's true that Astaire's 1933 screen test for RKO Pictures was deemed unimpressive, head of production David O. Selznick was convinced that the middle-aged hoofer with the big ears and weak chin had

Fred and Ginger in *Swing Time*, their sixth of ten films together. *Michael Ochs Archives/Getty Images*

charm that would translate to the screen. In Astaire's first picture for the studio, 1933's *Flying Down to Rio*, he had only fifth billing, but he was paired with a rising star named Ginger Rogers. For the rest of the 1930s, Fred and Ginger would be the first couple of filmdom.

Rogers was born Virginia McMath in 1911 in Independence, Missouri. Her mother left an abusive husband, briefly moved to Hollywood to be a screenwriter, and married a man named John Rogers. The family was living in Fort Worth, Texas, where Ginger's mother worked as a theater critic, when a vaudeville troupe led by Eddie Foy Sr. came through town and needed a last-minute stand-in. Rogers won a Charleston dance contest for the right to perform and ended up touring with Foy for six months.

She eventually made it to Broadway, where she danced in George and Ira Gershwin's *Girl Crazy* (1930), for which Astaire was a choreographer. Rogers became a star at nineteen and, three years before Astaire, was signed to a movie contract.

By the time they teamed up in *Flying Down to Rio*, Rogers had already acted in about twenty films—she famously sang the song "We're in the Money" in *Gold Diggers of 1933*—and as a result was billed above Astaire. But she had never danced with a partner before, and in the musical routines, he lifted her up to his level.

The breezy, escapist flick was a hit with the Depression-era audience, and Fred Astaire and Ginger Rogers went on to share top billing in eight other films for RKO: *The Gay Divorcee* (1934), *Roberta* (1935), *Top Hat* (1935), *Follow the Fleet* (1936), *Swing Time* (1936), *Shall We Dance* (1937), and *Carefree* (1938). (They reteamed in 1946 for the MGM musical *The Barkleys of Broadway*.) Although they were married to others—Astaire to socialite Potter, with whom he had two children, and Rogers to actor Lew Ayres—their on-screen connection seemed so genuine that the myth of their coupledom persists.

Astaire was a meticulous craftsman who planned his routines with choreographer Hermes Pan for months before the cameras rolled; as a result he made only a few movies each year (and earned a percentage of the profits). Meanwhile, Rogers made musicals and comedies with other co-stars, so that by the time she arrived for a shoot with Astaire, the dutiful (and presumably exhausted) Rogers had to hit the ground running. Although Astaire would work with some arguably better dancers, including Eleanor Powell, Ann Miller, and Cyd Charisse, he said that Rogers was the only one of his partners who never cried from the workload.

Unlike Fred Astaire, Ginger Rogers won an Oscar—for a drama, 1940's *Kitty Foyle*. A quarter century later, she was quoted in a magazine as saying that *Kitty Foyle* was her first movie. "It was my mother who made all those films with Fred Astaire."

Whether she actually said it has been disputed. Like so many Hollywood myths, there's no proof. ★

17

SPENCER TRACY AND KATHARINE HEPBURN

Why didn't the on-screen duo ever marry?

For more than a quarter century, Spencer Tracy and Katharine Hepburn were one of the most devoted couples in Hollywood, both on and off screen. But they never married, and the legend is that Tracy was such a steadfast Catholic that he refused to divorce the mother of his two children.

There's no question that Spencer Tracy was deeply and genuinely immersed in his faith. Although his mother was descended from the Protestant pilgrims who had founded Brown University, his father was a devout Irish Catholic. Born in Milwaukee in 1900, young Spencer was educated in Catholic schools. His father hoped the boy would become a priest.

After serving stateside in the Navy during World War I, Tracy lost his interest in joining the seminary, but not his interest in theology or his respect for priests (which he would often play in the movies). He briefly attended Ripon College in Wisconsin, then transferred to the American Academy of Dramatic Arts. Soon after his acceptance to the prestigious Manhattan school, he began appearing in Broadway productions, including *R.U.R.*, the sci-fi play that introduced the term "robot" to the English language.

In 1923, Tracy married actress Louise Treadwell, whom he had met during a stint with a Westchester acting troupe. She was not Catholic.

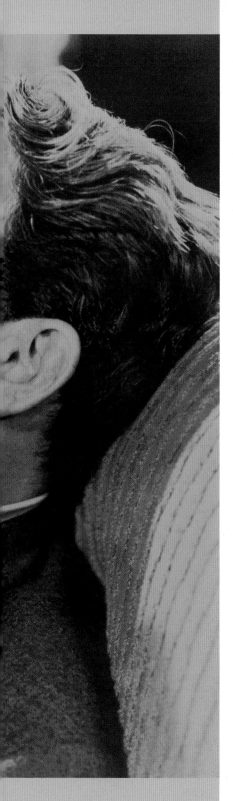

Soon Treadwell gave birth to a son named John. Ten months later, the couple discovered that their son was deaf. Treadwell had one more child with Tracy, a daughter also named Louise (and called Susie), but Treadwell was especially devoted to young John. In 1942, Treadwell started the John Tracy Clinic in Los Angeles to help other deaf children and their parents. Spencer Tracy was a major fundraiser during the clinic's early years, even though by then, he had long been absent from the family's home.

Tracy had moved the family to Hollywood in 1930. In 1933, he scored his first starring role, in *A Man's Castle*—and had an affair with his co-star, the very Catholic Loretta Young. A year later, Young issued a statement to the press lamenting that since she and Tracy could never be married in a religion that forbade divorce, they would stop seeing each other.

That didn't stop Tracy from having extramarital affairs.

In 1941, while Katharine Hepburn was riding high on the success of *The Philadelphia Story*, she requested that her co-star in an upcoming comedy called *Woman of the Year* be Spencer Tracy. She had never met the actor, but reportedly she had seen his Oscar-winning performance in *Captains Courageous* fifty-two times and felt that they would make a good team. Did they ever!

The chemistry between the plain-spoken Midwestern man and the outspoken daughter of Yankee intellectuals was obvious to the public—and to each other. Through nine

Spencer Tracy and Katharine Hepburn had immediate chemistry on the set of *Woman of the Year*, a comedy about married, headstrong journalists. *Hulton Archive/ Getty Images*

movies and twenty-six years together, Tracy and Hepburn (always billed in that order) were the living embodiment of the truism that opposites attract. On screen, they were verbally combative, with Hepburn representing the emancipated woman who would ultimately get her comeuppance from the no-nonsense man. Off screen, she doted on him, to the surprise of those who knew her.

Tracy was not Hepburn's first love. In 1928, she had married businessman Ludlow Ogden Smith. Although the marriage was brief, they remained lifelong friends. There is some evidence that she also had a romantic relationship with director John Ford. Like Tracy, Ford was a heavy drinker who brought out the maternal instincts in the otherwise independent Hepburn. When that relationship floundered, Hepburn lived for two years with aviator and film producer Howard Hughes, to whom she had been introduced by their mutual friend Cary Grant. But Tracy was the great, enduring love of her life.

Tracy continued to make public appearances with Treadwell, and he had an affair with Gene Tierney, his co-star in *The Plymouth Adventure* (1952). When his health deteriorated over the next decade, a result of his diabetes, drinking, and smoking, Hepburn was at his side. Insurance companies refused to cover Tracy's participation in the 1967 melodrama *Guess Who's Coming to Dinner*, so Hepburn pledged her own salary as collateral, believing that the job would keep Tracy alive a few months longer.

Two weeks after production wrapped, Tracy died of heart failure. He was in Hepburn's arms. She did not attend the funeral, out of respect for Treadwell.

The secret love affair became the subject of numerous articles and books. In a 1988 biography by Bill Davidson, Tracy is quoted as saying that the real reason he didn't marry Hepburn was not Catholicism but concern for his son John. According to the quote, by the time John was grown, the actor was such an alcoholic mess that Hepburn wouldn't marry him.

As Hepburn herself said of her longtime love, "Acting was easy for him. Life was the problem." ★

18

BOB HOPE
AND BING CROSBY

Were the on-screen treasure-hunters rich in real life too?

On screen they were rivals, a coward and a loafer who double-crossed each other over treasure maps, secret formulas, and Dorothy Lamour. But off screen, Bob Hope and Bing Crosby were two of the shrewdest businessmen in America. Together they would become multimillionaires.

Crosby was arguably America's first pop-music idol. Born Harry Lillis Crosby in Tacoma, Washington, in 1903, the laid-back baritone popularized jazz on the West Coast vaudeville circuit, first with the Paul Whiteman Orchestra and then as a solo performer. In 1931, he moved to Hollywood, where he thrived in radio, movies, and recorded music for more than twenty years. Crosby's 1942 recording of "White Christmas," a particular comfort to families separated by war, still remains the biggest-selling single of all time.

From 1940 to 1962, Crosby teamed with his best friend and golfing buddy, British-born comedian Leslie Townes "Bob" Hope, in seven "Road" comedies.

Hope's family had moved to the United States in 1908, when the boy was four. As a teenager the scrappy lad worked as a boardwalk barker, was briefly a boxer (under the pseudonym Packy East), and went to reform school. In the 1920s, he tried vaudeville, where he caught the eye of

silent-film star Fatty Arbuckle, who enlisted him as a performer for his theatre troupe. By the mid 1930s, Hope made it to Hollywood, and in 1940 he was teamed for the first time with the better-known Crosby.

In the gag-filled "Road" movies, the duo played song-and-dance men who looked for loot in the far corners of the world. In real life, Hope and Crosby were the epitome of the American dream.

The legend is that they once stood on a bluff in the Hollywood Hills, gazing out over the undeveloped land of the San Fernando Valley, and recognized the makings of another gold rush. They bought fruit orchards and vacant lots, and Crosby touted the new suburbia in his 1944 hit "The San Fernando Valley." When a Texas oil well in which they had invested paid off, Hope poured his profits into more land. By his own account he became the largest individual property owner in the state of California, with vast holdings in Palm Springs and Malibu.

Crosby invested in race horses, the first generation of audio and video tape recorders (which allowed him and Hope to pre-record, edit, and add laugh tracks to their radio and television programs), and frozen-food technology that squeezed extra profits from the orange groves. While Crosby was doing commercials for Minute Maid, he was the company's chairman of the board. Both actors bought stakes in major-league baseball teams, Hope in his boyhood hometown of Cleveland (where he had moved from London at the age of five), Crosby in Pittsburgh.

Although their off-screen friendship lent an authenticity to the "Road" repartee, in some significant ways, Hope and Crosby were very different from the characters they played in movies. Hope's trademark character was a coward, but in real life the comedian bravely entertained American troops in every major conflict from World War II to the Gulf War. And while Crosby had an easygoing persona and won an Oscar for playing a kindly priest in *Going My Way* (1944), at home he was a strict disciplinarian. His will stipulated that his children from two marriages could not inherit any of his considerable wealth until they were sixty-five. His oldest son, Gary, wrote a scathing tell-all book that accused his alcoholic father of physical and emotional abuse, and two of his other sons eventually committed suicide. For Crosby, the road to riches may not have been as smooth as it seemed. ★

Bob Hope, left, and Bing Crosby (with Dorothy Lamour) starred in seven "Road" films together from 1940 to 1962. *Redferns/Getty Images*

19

CARY GRANT
AND RANDOLPH SCOTT

Was their bachelor pad a private club with two members?

*F*ew Hollywood rumors are based on more open behavior than the alleged romance between Cary Grant and Randolph Scott.

No one has proven that the debonair Englishman and the American cowboy were lovers, but the clues were as big as *Life* magazine could print them.

Grant and Scott shared a seven-bedroom beach house for a decade, including during the brief stretch when Grant was married to actress Virginia Cherrill. Publicity photos of that era show the shirtless studs swimming together, jogging in the sand, and even feeding each other morsels. Cherrill, who played the blind flower girl in Charlie Chaplin's *City Lights*, may not have noticed the homoerotic glee in the buddy-buddy routine, but some journalists and other actors certainly did. Shortly after Grant and Scott met on the set of 1932's *Hot Saturday*, a press report dubbed them a "happy couple." Their mutual friend Carole Lombard quipped, "Their relationship is perfect. Randy pays the bills, and Cary mails them."

Cary Grant was born Archibald Leach in Bristol, England, in 1904. When his mother entered an asylum, young Archie ran off with an acrobatic troupe that eventually came to America. In New York, he shared a Greenwich Village apartment with fashion designer Jack Kelly (later known by his adopted professional name, Orry-Kelly). In 1932, the two men moved to Hollywood, where Mae West tapped the aspiring actor to co-star with her in *She Done Him Wrong*. But the trademark Cary Grant persona didn't develop until he acted opposite Katharine Hepburn in George Cukor's *Sylvia Scarlett*. The courtly Cukor, the godfather of gay Hollywood and the source for much of the speculation about Grant's sexuality, encouraged the handsome star to shake off his inhibitions.

Grant became a great comedian and an elegant charmer. In the screwball comedy *Bringing Up Baby* (1938), he may have been the first star to utter the word "gay" in its modern context. Caught wearing a pink nightgown, Grant's shy paleontologist says, "I just went gay all of a sudden." There is also a gay subtext to Grant's reaction to strapping athlete Scott in their one movie together, 1940's *My Favorite Wife*.

It was one of the last comedic roles for Scott, whose one hundred movies included sixty Westerns. Born in Virginia in 1898 and raised in North Carolina, he abandoned an engineering career when he discovered his love of theater and moved to California. His early patron in Hollywood was mogul Howard Hughes (who was also friends with Grant).

After meeting on the set of *Hot Saturday*, Scott and Grant lived together at three different addresses. Like Grant, Scott continued to live in the Malibu bachelor pad after he got married (to chemicals heiress Mariana duPont). The husband and wife were rarely seen in public together and divorced after three years. (A few years later Grant also married a fabulously wealthy woman, Woolworth heiress Barbara Hutton, also for three years.) In 1944, Scott married Patricia Stillman. That union lasted forty-three years and produced two children.

In 1948, Grant turned down a role in Alfred Hitchcock's *Rope*, a film that is often interpreted as having homoerotic undertones (although two years earlier he had starred in *Night and Day*, a biopic of gay icon Cole Porter, which portrayed the composer as a straight man).

In 1949, Grant married actress Betsy Drake. They remained together for a dozen years, and while she was uncertain about his past, she would later attest to their vigorous love life. It was Drake who convinced Grant to take the then-legal drug LSD to get in touch with his repressed feelings. Under a psychiatrist's supervision, he used the hallucinogen more than a hundred times.

After he retired from acting, Grant married twice more—to actress Dyan Cannon, with whom he had his only child (a daughter, Jennifer), and to hotel publicist Barbara Harris, who was forty-seven years his junior.

Unsurprisingly, the children of both Scott and Grant dispute that their fathers were gay or bisexual, despite testimony from friends like Cukor. Both actors said on many occasions that deceiving people was part of their job description. As the former Archie Leach said of his ex-wife Barbara Hutton, "She thought she was marrying Cary Grant." ★

Cary Grant, left, and
Randolph Scott at
"Bachelor Hall," the beach
house they shared, 1935.
*Hulton Archive/
Getty Images*

20

ROCK HUDSON
AND JIM NABORS

Were the invitations a joke—or a message from inside their closet?

Of all the ridiculous myths in Hollywood history, the one about Rock Hudson and Jim Nabors has turned out to be less ridiculous than most. The rumor that the heartthrob from the Doris Day movies and the hillbilly from *Gomer Pyle* were secretly married has persisted since the 1970s because it's based on a tiny kernel of truth. Hudson, as everyone now knows, was a closeted homosexual, and he and Nabors were indeed friends.

Gay Hollywood is a long-established, diverse community with its own traditions. Not surprisingly, those traditions include big parties hosted by wealthy, witty people who test the limits of "out" behavior. In the golden age of the studio system, the epicenter of gay Hollywood was the Brentwood home of George Cukor, director of *The Philadelphia Story* (1940). His weekly parties gathered homosexual luminaries such as Cole Porter, Noel Coward, and *Frankenstein* director James Whale, as well as sympathetic straight men and women like Humphrey Bogart and Katharine Hepburn. Yet in the movies themselves, open and positive depictions of gay life were almost non-existent.

During World War II, homosexual men served honorably (if not openly) in the Allied military forces, and after the war, sensitive actors such as Montgomery Clift—who was believed to have been bisexual—redefined American manhood. There were coded messages about homosexuality in movies from *Tea and Sympathy* (1956) to *Ben-Hur* (1959).

In the 1940s and 1950s, an agent named Henry Willson developed a stable of beefcake actors with monosyllabic names like Troy, Ty, and Clint. Although they posed as straight dreamboats, most of them were Willson's gay protégés. His prize specimen was a strapping lad from suburban Chicago named Roy Fitzgerald, who Willson renamed Rock Hudson. (Another one of Willson's clients, Tab Hunter, told me in a 2005 interview that when a magazine reporter learned that Hudson was gay, the agent offered gossip about Hunter in exchange for a promise to keep Hudson's sex life a secret.)

While Hunter maintained an off-screen relationship with Anthony Perkins, Hudson was forced to marry Willson's secretary, Phyllis Gates. The masquerade lasted three years, during which Hudson starred in a series of melodramas for Douglas Sirk (*Written on the Wind*) that are now regarded as camp classics.

After the divorce, Hudson enjoyed his greatest success, in three romantic comedies co-starring Doris Day: *Pillow Talk* (1959), *Lover Come Back* (1961), and *Send Me No Flowers* (1964). In retrospect the films are rife with hidden messages about Hudson's sexuality. For instance, in *Pillow Talk*, his tomcat character poses as an impotent mama's boy and Day's virginal character tries to seduce him. Later in the film, doctors are convinced he is pregnant.

In the wake of the civil rights struggles of the 1960s, gay men and women in major American cities became more open about publicly divulging their sexuality. Gay pride expressed itself in ways ranging from militancy to playfulness. One expression in the latter category was an annual party hosted by a middle-aged gay couple in the L.A. suburb of Huntington Beach. The satirical invitations, distributed widely to ensure a big turnout, boasted of special guests like the Queen of England.

In 1971, the invitation announced the upcoming nuptials of Rock Hudson and Jim Nabors, aka TV's Gomer Pyle. The announcement that the movie star would thereafter be known as "Rock Pyle" was a clue that the whole thing was a joke. But not everyone got it. The rumor was repeated by gossip columnists, deejays, even *Mad* magazine. Nabors, who was hosting a

"I am not happy that I have AIDS. But if that is helping others, I can at least know that my own misfortune has had some positive worth."

— Rock Hudson

TV variety show at the time, publicly denounced the "disgusting" stories. Hudson, who was playing a San Francisco police commissioner on the TV series *McMillan & Wife*, declined to comment.

Nabors and Hudson may well have been more than mere acquaintances. A photo from Hudson's estate shows Nabors visiting Rock on a movie set circa 1968; another depicts them attending a black-tie event together. They were both recurring guests on *The Carol Burnett Show*, and there are reports that they traveled together.

The irony is that after the prank that hinted at an enduring relationship, Nabors and Hudson could not risk being seen together. Unlike Burnett, Day, and Elizabeth Taylor, Nabors was not able to comfort or even acknowledge Hudson when the actor was dying a very public, tragic death. Hudson, the first major celebrity to announce a battle with AIDS, died in 1985 at age fifty-nine.

Jim Nabors, who sings "Back Home Again in Indiana" before each Indianapolis 500 car race, spends most of his time in Hawaii, where he owns a macadamia nut plantation. He has never married. ★

Carol Burnett with Rock Hudson, left, and Jim Nabors at the 1967 Academy Awards, four years before rumors of an impending marriage started circulating.
© Bettmann/Corbis

ELIZABETH TAYLOR AND RICHARD BURTON

21

Who was afraid of a rollercoaster love life?

They fought like cats and dogs and were hounded around the globe by the paparazzi that they themselves unleashed. But don't feel sorry for Elizabeth Taylor and Richard Burton. They had a ball.

Liz and Dick were the most famous and scandalous couple of the twentieth century. Between them they had thirteen marriages. They bankrupted a major studio, bought the world's most fabulous jewels, and were denounced by the Vatican for their "erotic vagrancy." Yet in the middle of this storm were two talented people who loved each other until their respective deaths.

Taylor's parents were Midwesterners, but baby Elizabeth waited until they were living in London, starting an art gallery for a rich uncle of Liz's father from St. Louis, before entering the world on February 27, 1932. She spent her childhood years in England. As war with Germany loomed, the Taylors moved to Hollywood, where Elizabeth's mother, a former stage actress, had family.

With her raven hair, violet eyes, and double rows of eyelashes (the result of a genetic mutation), Elizabeth caught the attention of casting directors, and she signed her first movie contract at age nine.

After the 1944 horse-racing movie *National Velvet*, Taylor transitioned into teen and adult roles, hitting her stride as a pampered fiancée in *Father of the Bride* (1950).

Liz and Dick (Elizabeth Taylor and Richard Burton) in Edinburgh in 1963. Taylor was married to Eddie Fischer until the following year. *Manchester Daily Express/SSPL via Getty Images*

Taylor's own marriages were front-page news. Her first was to hotel heir Nicky Hilton. The stormy marriage lasted less than a year. She then married milquetoast British actor Michael Wilding, with whom she had two sons.

During her brief marriage to Wilding, Taylor was cast opposite Montgomery Clift in *A Place in the Sun* (1951). It was Clift who encouraged Taylor to take her acting more seriously. In 1957, she earned the first of four consecutive Oscar nominations, opposite Clift in the Civil War romance *Raintree County*. Earlier that year she married producer Michael Todd, with whom she had a daughter. Todd died in a plane crash the following year. It was Taylor's only marriage not to end in divorce.

In 1959, Taylor fell in love with Todd's best friend, singer Eddie Fisher. At the time Fisher was married to beloved actress Debbie Reynolds, who had been Taylor's most recent maid of honor. The widowed Taylor was labeled a homewrecker when she married Fisher in May of that year.

"I don't pretend to be an ordinary housewife."

— Elizabeth Taylor

Taylor won the Best Actress Academy Award for her role as a high-class call girl in 1960's *BUtterfield 8*, an honor she called a pity prize after a serious bout with pneumonia. That year she became the highest-paid actress in the world when she signed a million-dollar contract to play the title role in the epic *Cleopatra*. Partly due to Taylor's lavish demands, which included a Roman villa for her human-and-animal entourage and daily deliveries of her favorite chili from Beverly Hills, the cost of the production ballooned to over $40 million—the equivalent of $300 million today. Adjusting for inflation, it was the most expensive movie ever made.

Although the three-hour film did reasonably well at the box office and was nominated for nine Oscars (and won four, in technical categories), it was so costly that it virtually bankrupted 20th Century Fox, which was forced to sell much of its back-lot real estate in west Los Angeles.

Today *Cleopatra* is best remembered as the movie where Liz met Dick.

Actually, Taylor had briefly met Burton at a Hollywood pool party in 1953, but she was not impressed with the unkempt Welsh actor. The son of a coal miner, Burton was born in Pontrhydyfen, Wales, in 1925. He won a scholarship to study at Oxford, served in the Royal Air Force during World War II, and was an acclaimed stage actor before entering movies.

Taylor and Burton began their "erotic vagrancy" on the set of *Cleopatra. 20th Century Fox/Getty Images*

On the Roman set of *Cleopatra*, Burton was determined to make Taylor another of his conquests, despite being married (to Welsh actress Sybil Williams) with two children. During the first love scene between Marc Antony and Cleopatra, the stars kept kissing after director Joseph L. Mankiewicz called "Cut." Their chemistry was palpable.

In a real sense, the couple's affair gave birth to the modern paparazzi

phenomenon. The term itself was coined around the time that production on *Cleopatra* was underway, by Italian director Federico Fellini, who named the gossip photographer in his 1960 movie *La Dolce Vita* "Paparazzo," the Italian word for a buzzing insect. Like the character, the real-life paparazzi prowled the fashionable Via Veneto, where Taylor and Burton often partied. The photographers would follow the stars on Vespa scooters to the villa where Burton and Fischer ultimately forced Taylor to choose sides.

She chose Dick.

When Burton traveled to Mexico to film an adaptation of Tennessee Williams' *Night of the Iguana* for director John Huston, Taylor followed. To the eternal delight of the Mexican tourism industry, Taylor and Burton bought adjoining villas in Puerto Vallarta (one of which is now a Liz-and-Dick-themed bed-and-breakfast where each room is named after one of their movies). They spent much of their courtship and subsequent marriage jetting around the world.

Nine days after Taylor's divorce from Fischer became final, she married Burton in Canada, where he was appearing in an acclaimed production of *Hamlet*. During the curtain call on the night of their marriage, he invited his new wife onto the stage and the Toronto audience went wild. In 1964, the couple adopted a German girl named Maria (whom Fisher had expected to raise).

Taylor continued to blossom as an actress, winning her second Oscar for co-starring with Burton in the 1966 drama *Who's Afraid of Virginia Woolf?*. Director Mike Nichols had intended to cast the more age-appropriate James Mason and Bette Davis in the roles of middle-aged married couple George and Martha, but like everyone else, he was mesmerized by the star power of Liz and Dick.

"She was the most sullen, uncommunicative, and beautiful woman I have ever seen."

— Richard Burton

Taylor and Burton would eventually star in six more movies together, almost all of them fatuous potboilers about feuding couples who resembled themselves. (Burton was nominated for six Academy Awards but never won, a record later bested by his boozy pal Peter O'Toole.) Although Burton was a hard drinker, Taylor could keep up with him, and unlike her husband, "One-Take Liz" almost never showed ill effects from her late-night carousing.

The battling Burtons divorced in 1974 after a turbulent decade of marriage. Taylor, raised in the studio system, dutifully released a statement to the fans of whom she was always mindful.

Those fans cheered when the couple remarried a year later in Africa. The second marriage ended after nine months.

In short order, Burton married model Susan Hunt and Taylor married

U.S. senator John Warner. In 1982, Taylor divorced Warner and coaxed the newly divorced Burton into co-starring in a stage production of Noel Coward's *Private Lives*. Despite bad reviews, the campy production about yet another feuding couple was a hit. In the middle of the play's run, Burton shocked Taylor by marrying Susan Hays, a humble production assistant he had met on the set of *Wagner* (1983), one of the many cheap European films he made after Hollywood stopped calling.

On August 5, 1984, Burton wrote a final love letter to Taylor in which he expressed his wish that they could be together again someday. A few hours after he mailed it, he died of a brain hemorrhage at his home in Switzerland. Burton was fifty-eight years old.

Taylor received the letter several days after the bad news. She kept it by her bedside through a quarter century marked by health problems, philanthropic outreach, and a brief marriage to construction worker Larry Fortensky, whom she met while at the Betty Ford Clinic. Elizabeth Taylor died in 2011 at age seventy-nine. ★

22

BRAD PITT
AND ANGELINA JOLIE

Is the first rule of family not to talk about family?

No couple since Liz and Dick has played the publicity game more effectively than Brad Pitt and Angelina Jolie. Their talent is undeniable, and their media savvy is incomparable. But if you try to suggest that they covet the attention, you might get sued.

Pitt and Jolie, indelibly dubbed "Brangelina" by the tabloid press, arrived at the summit of celebrity on different roads, Jolie from the high road of Hollywood privilege, Pitt from the low road of Midwestern dreams. Brad Pitt was born in Shawnee, Oklahoma, in 1963 and grew up in Springfield, Missouri. He attended the University of Missouri, where he was an advertising major in the journalism school, a popular member of a fraternity, and a model in the "Men of Mizzou" calendar.

In 1986, two credits short of graduation, Pitt took his life savings of $325, loaded his belongings into an old Datsun he called "Runaround Sue," and headed west on Route 66. He told his parents that he would be finishing college at an art school, but his secret hope was to parlay his good looks and country-boy charm into an acting career. "I never thought very far ahead," Pitt told me in a 2001 interview. "All I could think about was how much I loved movies."

Pitt bunked in North Hollywood with four friends from Missouri. One of his first jobs in Los Angeles was to wear a chicken suit outside an El Pollo Loco restaurant on Sunset Boulevard. That job lasted one day. So did his gig as a limo driver for a strip-o-gram service.

"Brangelina" at the premiere of *Salt* in 2010. *Photograph by Steve Granitz. WireImage/ Getty Images*

Pitt earned $38 as an extra in the movie *Less Than Zero* (1987), then landed recurring roles in the TV series *Dallas* and *Glory Days* before shooting to stardom with his breakthrough role as a larcenous hitchhiker in *Thelma & Louise* (1991). Buoyed by the attention, he starred in the low-budget cult film *Johnny Suede* in 1991 and the partially animated *Cool World* the following year. When Robert Redford cast the easy-going young actor in *A River Runs Through It* (1992), he seemed to be anointing Pitt as a possible successor to his own legacy—that of the blonde, all-American charmer.

Pitt stole *Interview with the Vampire* (1994) from star Tom Cruise, scored an international hit with David Fincher's *Se7en* in 1995, and earned an Oscar nomination as Best Supporting Actor for *Twelve Monkeys* (also 1995).

He dated actress Juliette Lewis and was engaged to Gwyneth Paltrow before meeting *Friends* star Jennifer Aniston while she was walking her beloved corgi Norman in Beverly Hills. Aniston and Pitt married in 2000 in a million-dollar ceremony, for which all the hired help had to sign non-disclosure agreements. During their five-year marriage, Pitt broke the bank with Steven Soderbergh's crime caper *Ocean's Eleven* (2001), was named *People* magazine's Sexiest Man Alive for a second time, and was cast in the 2005 spy spoof *Mr. & Mrs. Smith* opposite his female sex-symbol equivalent, Angelina Jolie.

Jolie is the daughter of Oscar winner Jon Voight (1978's *Coming Home*) and actress Marcheline Bertrand. Her parents separated in 1976, when she was a year old, and she was raised by her mother in New York and Los Angeles. As a teenager Jolie was a gloomy, black-clad loner who played with knives and aspired to be a funeral director. During the 1990s, she did some modeling on both sides of the Atlantic and appeared in music videos for Lenny Kravitz, Meat Loaf, and The Lemonheads.

She had roles in several TV movies, for which she replaced the surname Voight with her middle name, Jolie, partly in protest of her estranged father's infidelities. Jolie briefly married actor Jonny Lee Miller, won an Oscar of her own for her role as an institutionalized rebel in *Girl, Interrupted* (1999), and less briefly married actor Billy Bob Thornton, whose blood she wore in a vial around her neck as a token of their love. During that marriage, she adopted the first of her six (as of 2012) children, a Cambodian boy named Maddox she met while doing relief work for the United Nations.

Jolie reunited with her father in the 2001 hit *Lara Croft: Tomb Raider*, but soon denounced him publicly and legally changed her name. Yet a few years later she emulated Voight's recklessness by having an affair with Pitt, her married co-star. Jolie has said that the relationship didn't begin until Pitt's marriage was over, but their attraction on screen was undeniable.

In 2006, the couple had a biological child together, a daughter named Shiloh. (Earlier that year Pitt legally adopted both Maddox and Jolie's daughter Zahara, from Ethiopia.) To avoid press scrutiny, the child was born in Namibia. The parents sold the rights to the first photographs of her to *People* magazine for $4 million. They made a similar arrangement when they adopted a Vietnamese boy named Pax a year later.

Pitt and Jolie had twins, a boy named Knox and a girl named Vivienne, in 2008. This time the worldwide photo rights sold for an astounding $14 million, which went to the couple's charity, the Jolie-Pitt Foundation (which has contributed to tornado relief in Joplin, Missouri; a children's museum in Springfield, Missouri

; and housing, designed by Pitt, in flood-ravaged New Orleans).

As the couple built a family, Pitt built his reputation as a serious actor, with Oscar-nominated lead performances in 2008's *The Curious Case of Benjamin Button* and 2011's *Moneyball*. Jolie has excelled in action films such as *Wanted* (2008), earned an Oscar nomination for *Changeling* (2008), and made her directorial debut with the Bosnian war film *In the Land of Blood and Honey* (2011).

Pitt and Jolie are red-carpet perennials, but remarkably they don't have a publicist. They ration their interviews and have sued tabloids that violate their privacy. In 2010, the couple successfully sued Britain's *News of the World* for reporting that they were breaking up—then they donated the undisclosed settlement to their own charity. ★

PART 3
The Final CURTAIN

23

PEG ENTWISTLE

Did she jump or was she pushed?

When the body of actress Peg Entwistle was found on a Hollywood hilltop in 1932, her death came to symbolize the heartlessness of showbiz. But Entwistle was not an unknown actress desperate for work, and she did not jump from the now-famous Hollywood sign. The sign that towered above her body read "Hollywoodland," and in those days it had nothing to do with the industry that supposedly killed her.

Those last four letters were in place until 1949, seventeen years after Entwistle's death. The lighted sign had been erected in 1923 on the southern slope of Mount Lee in the Santa Monica Mountains, not to promote the film industry but to advertise the Hollywoodland real-estate development in a Los Angeles neighborhood called Beachwood Canyon. So while it's tempting to see the actress' death as a symbolic gesture toward the industry that supposedly spurned her, the truth is more complicated.

The actress, born Lillian Millicent Entwistle in Wales in 1908, lived with relatives in Beachwood Canyon for the last six months of her life while she tried to gain a foothold in the movies. She had come to California to act in a play called *The Mad Hope*s alongside Billie Burke (the Good Witch in *The Wizard of Oz*) and a promising young actor named Humphrey Bogart.

Entwistle had already been on Broadway—in fact, she had been in ten plays in just six years. Her famous co-stars included Lillian Gish, Henry Travers, and Robert Cummings. When Entwistle performed in a production

of Henrik Ibsen's *The Wild Duck*, it changed the life of a girl in the audience—a teenage Bette Davis told her mother "I want to be just like Peg Enwistle!" (A few years later, Davis herself would play the role of Hedvig.)

Entwistle earned consistently good reviews and toured the country on behalf of the prestigious Theatre Guild, a tour that was orchestrated by legendary playwright George Bernard Shaw.

During the successful L.A. run of *The Mad Hopes*, the orphaned Entwistle stayed with her aunt and uncle on Beachwood Avenue. Three days after the play closed, she was packing to return to New York when she

The *New York Times* headline on September 19, 1932, declared, "Actress Ends Life by Jumping Off Fifty-Foot Sign After Failure in the Movies." *Copyright Bettman / Corbis / AP Images*

received a call from RKO Pictures, which offered her a screen test. The studio was impressed by the blonde-haired, blue-eyed ingénue and signed her for David O. Selznick's supernatural mystery *13 Women*, starring Irene Dunne and Myrna Loy. But when the movie previewed, the audience was disturbed by Entwistle's character, a vengeful lesbian, and much of her role was trimmed from the final cut of the film.

On the day the movie officially opened, September 16, 1932, Entwistle told her aunt and uncle she was going to meet some friends. She is alleged to have traveled up Beachwood Avenue to Mount Lee, a four-mile journey on winding roads with no sidewalks, followed by a canyon thick with brush and rattlesnakes. She wore high heels the whole way. Because of the difficulty of the trip; the fact that there were many taller buildings closer to her house; and the testimony from a caretaker living near the Hollywoodland sign, who said he never saw her, author Leo Braudy has speculated that Entwistle was murdered downhill and that her body was arranged to look like a suicide. (And if Entwistle did jump, there is no evidence that she jumped from the unlucky thirteenth letter, a legend concocted in a well-known Hollywood scandal book. The utility ladder was behind the H.)

Two days later, a hiker walking below the H found a body and a nearby purse containing an apparent suicide note. It read: "I am afraid I am a coward. I am sorry for everything. If I had done this a long time ago, it would have saved a lot of pain. P. E." A local newspaper printed the note and the news about the unidentified woman. Entwistle's uncle deduced that it was Peg.

But had she committed suicide over a stalled career? Or was the note in her purse a break-up letter that was never delivered?

Entwistle had only been in Hollywood for six months, a mere blink in the life of an experienced actress who was presumably accustomed to auditions and rejections. And in another contradiction to the legend, Entwistle's surviving relatives have said that RKO had renewed her contract.

So maybe the real reason pertained to her personal life.

In 1927, Entwistle had married an older New York writer and actor named Robert Keith. But the marriage dissolved when she found out he had a litigious ex-wife and a son, both of whom were owed money. Even in the midst of their divorce, Entwistle helped Keith pay off his debts. It is not unreasonable to think that romantic woes and Depression-era economics were the real villains that drove the twenty-four-year-old actress to her death.

There is one final irony (and it isn't the unsubstantiated report that a job offer was in the mail on the day she died). Robert Keith's son Brian—Entwistle's stepson—would himself grow into an accomplished actor. Brian Keith, star of the original *Parent Trap* and television's *Family Affair*, followed in his stepmother's footsteps. In 1997, just two months after daughter Daisy committed suicide, Keith was found dead of a self-inflicted gun shot. ★

24

JAMES DEAN

Was he too fast—or too unlucky?

*T*he car accident that killed James Dean was not his fault. And contrary to legend, he probably wasn't speeding.

Marlon Brando changed acting, but James Dean changed the way people lived. When he died on September 30, 1955, he was just twenty-four years old. Only one of the three movies in which he starred, *East of Eden* (1955), had been released in theaters. Yet his afterlife would include two posthumous Oscar nominations and a generation of fans who embraced the motto he personified: "Live fast, die young."

Dean had already competed on several racing tracks in Southern California when he signed on for the 1956 epic *Giant*. During the making of that film, he was contractually forbidden to race and he filmed a public service announcement with fellow actor Gig Young that advised young drivers to slow down. "The life you save might be mine," Dean said.

On September 22, 1955, Dean completed work on *Giant* and picked up a four-cylinder Porsche Spyder he had purchased a few months earlier, one of only ninety built. He nicknamed it "The Little Bastard." The next day, he met and gave a joyride to Hollywood newcomer Alec Guinness. Guinness is said to have predicted that Dean would be dead in a week.

On the morning of September 30, three days after attending a preview screening for *Rebel Without a Cause* (which he had filmed before *Giant*), Dean and his mechanic, Porsche employee Rolf Wütherich, headed north to a road rally in Salinas, California. Behind them, in Dean's station wagon, were his friend Bill Hickman and photographer Sanford Roth. South of Bakersfield, Dean was ticketed for going 65 miles per hour in a 55 miles per hour zone. The last autograph he ever gave was on the ticket he signed for the highway patrolman.

At the Y-shaped intersection of Highways 466 and 41 near Cholame, a college student named Donald Turnupseed turned left across the lane in which Dean was driving straight. Because the silver Porsche was so low to the ground, Turnupseed may not have seen it. His Ford sedan struck the convertible at a forty-five-degree angle and demolished it. Wütherich was thrown from the vehicle and Dean was found gravely injured in the passenger seat (reinforcing an unproven story, told by an eyewitness, that Dean had not been driving). Roth snapped pictures as Dean was pulled from the car.

Dean was rushed to a hospital in Paso Robles, where he died that evening. Wütherich was hospitalized for months before he returned home to Germany. Turnupseed was not seriously injured, nor was he ticketed. For the rest of his long life, he refused to talk about the crash.

A highway patrolman at the scene estimated from the damage that the Porsche had been going 55 miles per hour. A 2005 forensic re-enactment for *National Geographic* estimated the speed to have been between 63 and 75 miles per hour. Fast, but not the stuff of legend.

Yet when *Rebel Without a Cause* was released a few weeks later, Dean was instantly elevated from a promising actor to the embodiment of a young outlaw, a role reinforced by the supposed recklessness of his death. It's a dubious legacy, and one that overshadows his considerable

James Dean on the set of *Giant*, circa 1955. *Hulton Archive/Stringer/ Getty Images*

talent. In his three films and in several TV dramas (including one in which he played a fugitive who terrorizes a country doctor played by Ronald Reagan), Dean combined the physical intensity of Marlon Brando with the introspection of Montgomery Clift. He was a cunning actor who could steal a scene with a gesture, like the rope trick he performed in *Giant*. Though his improvisations drove directors crazy, they were both daring and deeply rooted in the characters he played.

Dean's methodology and moody persona have influenced generations of actors, from Paul Newman (who did an unsuccessful screen test with Dean for *East of Eden* and inherited Dean's intended role in 1956's *Somebody Up There Likes Me*) to Martin Sheen (who collects Dean memorabilia) to Johnny Depp (who hosted a BBC radio documentary to mark the fiftieth anniversary of Dean's death). The aura of rebellion resonated with musicians too: Elvis Presley studied James Dean, John Lennon said the Beatles wouldn't have existed without him, and a teenage Bob Dylan bought a red jacket so he could look like Dean's character in *Rebel Without a Cause*.

While the whereabouts of the original red jacket, and those of the parts that were cannibalized from the Porsche and installed in other ill-fated cars, are still hotly debated, many other artifacts from Dean's life are on display in Fairmount, Indiana, where he was raised (after being born in nearby Marion, Indiana, in 1931) and is buried. At the Fairmount Historical Museum, pilgrims can see his bongo drums, watch the animated movie he produced about bullfighting, and read the yearbook from the high school where the bespectacled youth discovered acting. At the nearby gift shop, tell-all books by alleged lovers of both sexes wrestle over his legacy.

On the last weekend of every September, thousands of fans in 1950s regalia descend on Fairmount for the annual James Dean Festival. There's a lookalike contest and sometimes even a re-enactment of the cliff-top car race from *Rebel*. The most devoted fans participate in a candlelight walk from the Quaker church that hosted Dean's funeral to the graveyard where his frequently stolen headstone is adorned with cigarettes and love letters.

Dean had a knack for befriending photographers, and, unlike Elvis, he never devolved from a beautiful youth to an aging parody of himself. What fans mourn is not only the death of a talented young actor but the possibility that this rebel could have kept driving toward something bigger. ★

25

GEORGE REEVES

Did Superman surrender to despair?

One of the first Hollywood myths I heard in the schoolyard was that the actor who played Superman on TV committed suicide by trying to fly out of a skyscraper window. But George Reeves didn't jump to his death, and there's reasonable doubt as to whether he committed suicide at all.

George Brewer was born in Iowa in 1914. After his parents split up and his mother remarried, he was adopted by his stepfather, renamed George Bessemer, and raised in Pasadena, California. His talent was evident during performances at the Pasadena Playhouse, which led to a contract with Warner Bros. and, from there, his first credited movie role in *Gone with the Wind* (1939). Billed as George Reeves, he was in the first scene of the movie, playing one of the red-haired Tarleton twins. He and actor Fred Crane are chatting with Vivien Leigh (as Scarlett O'Hara) when she utters her famous line, "Fiddle-dee-dee. War, war, war. This war talk's spoiling all the fun at every party this spring."

A role in the biggest movie of all time, plus his marriage to actress Ellanora Needles a year later, should have been the beginning of great things for Reeves. Then the war broke out. He still managed to act in some serials, and he won acclaim for his performance in the battlefield drama *So Proudly We Hail*, but in 1943 he was drafted. He served in the U.S. Army Air Force and in the Army Motion Picture Unit.

After the war, film work was scarce, so in 1949 he briefly tried television in New York. Around this time, shortly after separating from his wife, Reeves met and fell in love with Toni Mannix, the wife of ruthless MGM executive Eddie Mannix. With Eddie's implicit consent, Toni supported Reeves financially while the fitness buff auditioned for films. In 1951, he was offered the lead in a B-movie called *Superman and the Mole Men*, which was immediately spun into a TV series about a crime-fighting visitor from another planet,

disguised as mild-mannered reporter Clark Kent. (Superman had been introduced to the American public in 1933 in a short story by writer Jerry Siegel, who co-created the character with illustrator Joe Shuster.)

The TV show *Adventures of Superman* was a hit with kids, and Reeves became one of the most famous men in America (and a tireless worker on behalf of children's charities). But he was paid only during the eight weeks per year that the show was in production, and restrictive contracts prevented him from starring in any films. He did have a small supporting role in the Oscar-winning *From Here to Eternity* (1953)—it's not true that the part was trimmed after preview audiences snickered at the sight of Superman—but Reeves wanted more from his career. He toured in a musical variety show with some of his TV co-stars and started his own production company.

In 1958, Reeves split from Mannix, became engaged to a young socialite named Leonore Lemmon, and stepped behind the camera to direct a few episodes of *Superman*. In 1959, the series was renewed for another year, and Reeves was said to be looking forward to a summer publicity tour in Australia. But on June 16, while Lemmon and some friends partied in his Benedict Canyon home, Reeves left the group and went upstairs. He was later found dead, of a single gunshot wound to the head.

The coroner ruled it a suicide, as the naked body in the bedroom had a gun at its feet. But some things didn't add up. Lemmon and her drunken houseguests waited forty-five minutes to call the police and couldn't get their stories straight on how they had spent the evening. No fingerprints were found on the gun. An empty shell casing was under the body. And there were two other bullet holes in the floor of the room.

The case has been the subject of books and of the 2006 movie *Hollywoodland*, starring Ben Affleck as Reeves. The movie hedges its bets, offering evidence that Reeves was murdered by one of the Mannixes, and counter-evidence that he died in a drunken tussle with Lemmon (a position supported by Reeves' friend and *Gone with the Wind* co-star Fred Crane), but it finally ascribes the death to a simple suicide.

The key to the mystery may be Eddie Mannix. He was Hollywood's "fixer" when bad publicity threatened a studio investment—he is suspected of covering up the murder of Jean Harlow's husband Paul Bern (which was also ruled a suicide) and the beating to death of *Three Stooges* founder Ted Healy (possibly by actor Wallace Beery, whom MGM immediately sent overseas). Mannix's wife Toni had become obsessed with Reeves after their breakup and was distraught about his upcoming marriage. Eddie was a philanderer, but he wanted to keep his wife happy. With his mob, police, and press connections, he was perfectly positioned to get away with murder.

Plus, Reeves' will named Toni Mannix, not Leonora, as his beneficiary.

TV's Superman was cremated and buried in a vault in Pasadena. His death remains an unsolved Hollywood mystery. ★

George Reeves' death at forty-five remains an unsolved Hollywood mystery. *Hulton Archive/ Stringer/Getty Images*

26

CARL SWITZER

Was the Little Rascal dogged by misfortune?

When he was just seven years old, Carl Switzer became famous for his portrayal of button-nosed, squeaky-voiced Alfalfa in the *Our Gang* serials. Despite popular belief, Alfalfa wasn't the only role Switzer ever played, and were it not for a tardy paycheck from a prestigious movie, he might have had a long, prosperous acting career—instead of being killed at age thirty-one.

Switzer was born in 1927 in Paris, Illinois, where freckle-faced Carl and his older brother Harold were celebrated for their musical talents. On a sightseeing trip to Hollywood in 1934, the Switzer family visited the Hal Roach Studios, which made Will Rogers and Laurel & Hardy household names. In the cafeteria, Carl and Harold launched into an impromptu dance routine. Roach liked what he saw and signed the brothers for his *Our Gang* series.

While Harold was soon relegated to the background, Carl flourished in the recurring role of the gawky, cowlicked, and melodically challenged Alfalfa.

On the set, Switzer developed a reputation as a temperamental brat and practical joker. Robert Blake, who played Mickey (and would grow up to star in the television series *Baretta* and be tried for his wife's murder), recalled how Switzer used bubblegum to sabotage the equipment of a cameraman who had hurried him. To get even with a hostile director, Switzer once urinated on some hot studio lights, causing a literal stink that required the set to be evacuated.

Switzer appeared in more than sixty *Our Gang* shorts between 1935 and 1940, but by age twelve he was deemed too old to continue. (He was not entitled to residuals when the series was renamed *Little Rascals* and syndicated to television.) He went on to have small roles in several memorable films, including *Going My Way*, *Pat and Mike*, *The High and the Mighty*, and *It's a Wonderful Life* (in which he played the jilted suitor who opens the dance floor beneath Jimmy Stewart and Donna Reed). He also did some acting on his godfather's television series, *The Roy Rogers Show*.

In 1959, Switzer had finished work on the jailbreak movie *The Defiant Ones* with Sidney Poitier and Tony Curtis. As he waited for a paycheck and career resurgence from the film, he did part-time work for his godfather as a guide for Rogers' bear-hunting operation. When one of the hunting dogs he had borrowed from a roughneck named Bud Stiltz broke free, Switzer offered a cash reward for its return. A few days later, a man brought the dog to the bar where Switzer sometimes worked. Switzer paid him the $35 reward and gave him another $15 worth of free drinks.

Switzer soon determined that Stiltz should have reimbursed him for the reward money. On January 21, 1959, Switzer and his photographer friend Jack Piott arrived drunk at Stiltz's house in the San Fernando Valley to settle the matter.

There are differing accounts of what happened next from Piott, Stiltz, and Stiltz's then-teenage stepson Thomas Corrigan (whose mother had jilted cowboy star Crash Corrigan to be with Stiltz). Piott claimed that when Stilz's wife allowed him and Switzer to enter the house, Piott ran in and smacked Stiltz with a desk clock. Stiltz ran for a gun, which went off during the struggle, fatally wounding Switzer. Stiltz testified that Switzer brandished an open switchblade. But young Corrigan told police that his stepfather had answered the door with a gun in his hand and shot Switzer, who dropped a tiny penknife from his pocket as he bled to death from a bullet to the abdomen. And indeed, detectives found a closed penknife beneath Switzer's body.

At the homicide trial, Stiltz was acquitted on the grounds of self-defense.

The killing of Carl Switzer generated little publicity, perhaps because it coincided with the death of Cecil B. DeMille—who had directed Switzer in *The Ten Commandments* (1956). The man who would always be remembered as little Alfalfa was buried in the Hollywood Memorial Park Cemetery. The grave marker includes a picture of a spotted canine, which might represent Petey, the mascot of *Our Gang*—or that damn hunting dog. ★

Carl Switzer, left, with Darla Hood and "Spanky" (George McFarland) in 1936, was a notorious prankster on the *Our Gang* set. *Getty Images*

27

MARILYN MONROE

Was the love goddess a lonely suicide?

*T*he legend has grown like Rapunzel's hair. A fair maiden, imprisoned in a tower where she would never lose her beauty, drank a deadly potion as her only escape. But there's compelling evidence that Marilyn Monroe didn't deliberately wash down a fatal dose of pills and that ,instead, she died at the hands of a visitor.

The death of Marilyn Monroe is as fishy as the death of John F. Kennedy—and involved some of the same people.

At this point, there's no denying that the president and the movie star were lovers. Reliable sources say they had a tryst at Bing Cosby's house in Palm Springs in the spring of 1962. For Monroe, a liaison with the president of the United States was the icing on a layer cake that also included marriages to America's most beloved sports hero (Joe DiMaggio) and most esteemed playwright (Arthur Miller). Whether Robert Kennedy was also on the dessert cart or was just a busboy sent to clean up his brother's mess is almost beside the point. In the last months of her life, Monroe was involved with some very important—and very dangerous—people.

In thirty-six years, she had come a long way. She was born Norma Jeane Mortenson in Los Angeles on June 1, 1926. Her mother was a divorced movie editor whose married name was Gladys Baker, and Norma Jeane grew up with that surname instead of Mortenson, which was the name of one of Gladys' boyfriends. Norma Jeane's real father may have actually

Norma Jeane Baker, circa 1941. *Silver Screen Collection/Getty Images*

been a man named Stanley Giffords, whom she later described as looking like Clark Gable in the one photograph she was shown. For the rest of her short and troubled life, she would seek father figures.

Gladys was troubled too, and while she spent time in mental institutions, Norma Jeane lived with foster parents and in an orphanage near Paramount Studios. At sixteen, she married a twenty-one-year-old merchant marine named James Dougherty. While he was serving in the Pacific, Norma Jeane worked at a munitions factory, where she was photographed for a spread in *Yank* magazine. The photographer suggested she sign up with a modeling agency, and soon the natural brunette with the bleach-lightened hair became a popular cover girl. When Dougherty saw one of her photos in a men's magazine, he ordered her to quit modeling. Instead she divorced him.

Norma Jeane caught the eye of an executive at 20th Century Fox, who signed her to a contract for $125 a week. He also advised her to change her first name to Marilyn. Following the example of her idol Jean Harlow, she adopted her mother's maiden name, Monroe.

Marilyn Monroe had single scenes in a handful of movies that were released in 1948, by which time she had already been dropped by the studio and had posed for nude photos to pay the rent. She signed a six-month contract with Columbia Pictures, which gave her second billing in a musical called *Ladies of the Chorus* (1948)—and then dropped her when she refused the advances of studio chief Harry Cohn. As a freelancer, she wiggle-walked through a scene in the Marx Brothers' *Love Happy* (1949), which attracted the influential agent Johnny Hyde. Hyde paid for cosmetic surgery to Monroe's nose and chin and landed her showcase roles in the prestige films *The Asphalt Jungle* and *All About Eve* (both 1950).

"Being a sex symbol is a heavy load to carry, especially when one is tired, hurt, and bewildered."

— Marilyn Monroe

By 1952, Monroe had been a presenter at the Academy Awards, appeared on the covers of *Life* and *Look* magazines, and started dating baseball star DiMaggio. She was hardly an unknown when a new magazine called *Playboy* reprinted one of her nude photos as its debut centerfold in December 1953.

Monroe's relationship with DiMaggio, made official at San Francisco City Hall in January 1954, coincided with her ascendancy as Hollywood's top sex symbol. DiMaggio wanted her to retire and have babies. Instead, she spent their honeymoon entertaining U.S. troops in Korea. A few months later, when he watched Manhattan bystanders hoot as Monroe filmed the billowing-dress scene from 1955's *The Seven Year Itch*, the marriage was effectively over. In the wake of their divorce, Monroe moved to New York, studied at the Actors Studio, and started dating Miller, whom she had known socially since 1950.

Around the time that Monroe gave one of her best performances, as a small-time singer in *Bus Stop* (1956), her boyfriend Miller was called to testify before the House Un-American Activities Committee. Studio executives urged her to end the relationship. Instead, they married, in June 1956. Miller refused to testify about communist subversion and was threatened with prison. During this period, Monroe suffered a miscarriage. She took a two-year hiatus from acting, returning in 1959 to star in her greatest success, Billy Wilder's comedy *Some Like It Hot*.

Miller wrote the latter-day Western *The Misfits* as a valentine for his wife. It was filmed in 1960 near Reno, Nevada. During the arduous production, which would be the final film for co-star Clark Gable, the marriage foundered. In 1961 an exhausted Monroe checked into a New York psychiatric hospital. Forbidden to leave, she was locked in a ward with incurable psychotics. For help she turned to DiMaggio, with whom she had remained close.

Monroe returned to Los Angeles and became involved with both President Kennedy and singer Frank Sinatra. A common denominator between Sinatra and Kennedy was actor Peter Lawford, a member of Sinatra's "Rat Pack" who was married to Kennedy's sister, Patricia. His activities in the summer of 1962 are a key to unlocking the mystery of Monroe's death.

Sinatra had been a staunch supporter of Kennedy during his presidential campaign. Sinatra's friend, Chicago mob boss Sam Giancana, had pulled some dubious strings to help Kennedy win the state of Illinois and thus the presidency. But after the election, the new president and his brother, Attorney General Robert Kennedy, did not just distance themselves from the mobsters who had known the Kennedys since the days when their father was a bootlegger—they actively prosecuted them.

There is evidence that Sinatra and Lawford passed messages—and warnings—between the two camps. Longtime FBI director J. Edgar Hoover, who wanted blackmail material to ensure he kept his job, eavesdropped on the various parties, including Monroe. But while Hoover hated the Kennedys, he was soft on organized crime. In the 1940s and 1950s, he denied that such a thing as the Mafia existed, even as he secretly enlisted mobsters to help him fight communism.

While Monroe was filming 1962's *Something's Got to Give*—her last film, which would have included her first nude scene—her modest home in Brentwood was bugged. (In 1972, TV actress Veronica Hamel bought and renovated the house, where she found surveillance equipment hidden in almost every room.) While it's unclear whether the bugs had been planted by Hoover's FBI or by henchmen of Giancana and Teamsters boss Jimmy

Hoffa, there is no question that her relationship with the Kennedys was attracting unwanted attention. Shortly after Monroe sang "Happy Birthday, Mr. President" at Madison Square Garden while dolled up in the tightest possible dress, furious executives at Fox Studios fired her from the movie.

Phone records for June and July indicate that Monroe made many calls to the White House and to Robert Kennedy's office at the Justice Department. Those closest to RFK insist that the father of seven was a loyal husband and that his friendship with Monroe merely entailed political discussions. But some investigators, including Anthony Summers in his well-researched 1985 book *Goddess*, suggest that Robert Kennedy had replaced his older brother in Monroe's bed, citing witness reports that he flew by helicopter into Los Angeles on the day of her death. That has led to speculation that Monroe was murdered by Kennedy operatives or by the Attorney General himself after she threatened to reveal the affair(s).

Another possibility is that henchmen of Hoover or Giancana murdered Monroe to implicate the Kennedys. A *third* possibility is that Dr. Ralph Greenson, Monroe's trusted psychiatrist, accidentally overdosed the drug-dependent actress and then tried to cover it up. Given the evidence, of all the possible scenarios, suicide seems the least likely.

Here's a timeline from the last day of Monroe's life.

After a typically sleepless night, she spent the afternoon of August 4 in session with Dr. Greenson, a controlling figure who had hired housekeeper Eunice Murray to keep an eye on Monroe for him. It's possible that Monroe may have discussed terminating her arrangements with Greenson and Murray, at the behest of DiMaggio. (Some investigators believe that Monroe and DiMaggio had reconciled and even discussed remarriage.) Friends who saw Monroe after her marathon session with Greenson reported that she seemed distraught.

Lawford called her house in the late afternoon and invited her to a dinner party where he was expecting Warren Beatty, Natalie Wood, and possibly Robert Kennedy, who may have hurried down from an event in San Francisco. (Former L.A. Police Chief Darryl Gates is among those who believe the Attorney General was in town that day, and a Beverly Hills cop reported pulling over a speeding car containing Kennedy, Lawford, and Greenson.) Monroe declined the invitation. Around 7:15 p.m. she spoke with Joe DiMaggio Jr., her former stepson, about his recent breakup with a woman Monroe didn't like.

Marilyn in costume for the Western *River of No Return* in January 1954, the same month she eloped with Joe DiMaggio. *Hulton Archive/ Getty Images*

Although DiMaggio Jr. later told investigators that she seemed to be in a good mood, Lawford reported that half an hour later, when he called her with another invitation to the party, Monroe sounded drugged and told him to bid farewell to the President on her behalf. Then the phone line went dead. As later evidence suggests, Lawford may have fabricated some of those details.

Lawford then called his lawyer to express his concern for Marilyn's well-being. Lawford's lawyer called Marilyn's lawyer, who called Murray. She reported (or assumed) that Monroe was fine. Around 10, Lawford called two of Monroe's neighbors who had just returned home from his party, but soon he called them back to say that Dr. Greenson was handling the situation.

Here's where the accounts get hopelessly tangled. Murray later claimed that she called Dr. Greenson around 3 a.m., after she noticed a light (or a phone cord) beneath Monroe's locked door. Murray said she went to the outside of the house and saw through a window that Monroe was unconscious. The doctor rushed over, broke the window to enter the room, and confirmed that Monroe was dead. The police officially arrived at 4:30 a.m.

Yet Monroe's studio publicist was notified of her death as early as 10:30 p.m., while he was attending a concert at the Hollywood Bowl.

An ambulance company owner and driver reported that an ambulance arrived at the house before midnight, took Monroe to a hospital, then returned with the dead body.

When police arrived at the house, they found shattered glass outside the bedroom window, indicating it had been broken from the inside. Monroe's nude body was lying face down on her bed, with a phone in her hand. Rigor mortis had already set in, indicating that she had been dead for about six hours.

Curiously, when the police arrived, Murray was doing a load of laundry.

The autopsy was performed by the soon-to-be-famous Dr. Thomas Noguchi, who ruled the cause of death a "probable suicide" from a barbiturate overdose. (Noguchi would perform the autopsy on RFK six years later.) But so many questions were raised by the rushed autopsy that Noguchi himself would eventually call for a re-examination. Although more than a dozen pill bottles were found by Monroe's bed, there was no empty glass, and Monroe did not have a water source in the bedroom. No pill-capsule residue or dye was found in Monroe's stomach. Her liver contained the equivalent of fifty sedatives—enough to induce vomiting and cause her to drop the phone. Most tellingly, she had inflammation of the rectum, indicating a forced enema.

Lawford, who rushed to the scene with private eye and wire-tapper Fred Otash the next morning (after which the locked file cabinet containing Monroe's journal was found busted open), would eventually tell his third wife, Deborah Gould, that Monroe had died from an anal injection.

Many pathologists agree that the fatal drugs were probably administered via an enema, but in the past half century, scores of investigators have argued over who did the honors. One tragic theory is that Greenson enlisted Murray to sedate Monroe with chloral hydrate, unaware that the actress had already taken enough nembutal earlier in the day to cause a fatal interaction.

A more sinister theory places the blame on Robert Kennedy. The decidedly shifty Murray would eventually claim that Kennedy and Lawford had visited the house that evening and ordered the housekeeper to leave. Monroe's next-door neighbor, who was hosting a bridge party, also claimed that Kennedy visited the house, and Lawford's neighbor in Santa Monica claimed that a helicopter took someone from the beach that night.

There's also a theory that Monroe was killed because she was divulging secrets to Sinatra (and thus Giancana) about the Kennedys' Cuba policy or prosecutions against Mob figures. That might explain why FBI agents seized Monroe's phone records from the local Pacific Bell office within hours of her death. (Those records then vanished, as did the original police and autopsy reports.)

Or maybe it was a warning from enemies that JFK and RFK could be the next to die.

Each of these theories is bolstered by disinterested witnesses and unearthed evidence. Yet still there are those who refuse to look past the conventional wisdom that Marilyn Monroe committed suicide—just as there are those who think JFK was later struck by the most gymnastic and durable bullet in the history of forensics, fired by a leftist loner with no spy-agency background, who in turn was murdered by a patriotic strip-club owner with no Mob connections. For those people, we recommend a library card. ★

SHARON TATE

Was Manson the murderer—or merely a bad influence?

*C*harles Manson gets more mail than any other prisoner in the United States. But if you could get him to answer your letter, he would tell you what he's been saying for more than forty years: he didn't kill Sharon Tate, and he didn't kill any of her houseguests. He wasn't even there when the murders happened.

And he would be telling the truth.

Manson was convicted on seven counts of conspiracy relating to a two-day killing spree in August 1969. While he was undoubtedly the mastermind, he did not wield the murder weapons.

Depending on your point of view, the most infamous thrill killings in American history were either senseless crimes, tragic consequences of one man's lousy childhood, or the logical results of the 1960s social experiment.

Charles Manson was born in Cincinnati, Ohio, in 1934, to a hard-drinking teenage mother who would soon serve time for robbing a gas station. Little Charlie was raised by an aunt and uncle in West Virginia. By the time he was a teenager, he was bouncing through the penal system on burglary and car-theft charges. In March 1967, when he was ordered to be released from a California prison after serving time for check fraud, pimping, and parole violations, Manson asked to stay in his cell but was turned down. At age thirty-two, he had spent half his life behind bars, and the outside world was changing rapidly.

Manson headed for San Francisco, where the Summer of Love was about to bloom. The charismatic conman wasn't peddling peace, yet a small flock of flower children clutched his bouquet of psychedelic drivel to their bosoms. By the end of that watershed year, self-styled guru Manson and his mostly female "Family" were traveling up and down the West Coast in a converted school bus.

Their travels took them to Los Angeles, where Manson hoped to become a rock star. In prison he had learned to play guitar, and he envisioned the Family as a musical troupe. (It's a myth, however, that Manson auditioned for *The Monkees*. He was still in prison when that show was cast.) Through the girls, he befriended Beach Boys drummer Dennis Wilson. Manson and at least a dozen of his followers moved into Wilson's Sunset Boulevard home, where the girls acted as servants. Wilson paid for Manson to record demo versions of some songs and introduced him to friends in the entertainment industry, including record producer Terry Melcher and business manager Rudi Altobelli. Before long, Manson and his Family were on the move again, having been kicked out of the Sunset Boulevard house by Wilson's manager. This time they were accompanied by a young Texan named Charles Watson, who had once picked up a hitchhiking Wilson.

Sharon Tate with husband Roman Polanski in 1969, months before the Manson murders. *AFP/Getty Images*

They headed to the Spahn Ranch, a former movie locale on the outskirts of Los Angeles, and two other ranches near Death Valley, where Family members did chores in exchange for free rent. The LSD-addled Manson soon became convinced that the United States was on the verge of a race war. In the Beatles' song "Helter Skelter" he heard a coded message urging him to incite violence and preside over the wreckage. He began writing songs that he expected would start the revolution.

On March 23, 1969, Manson went looking for Terry Melcher, who had missed an appointment to come listen to Manson's new material. Melcher had been renting a house at 10050 Cielo Drive in Benedict Canyon in Los Angeles. A photographer stopped Manson in the house's driveway and told him that Melcher had moved out. Peering through the front curtains was twenty-six-year-old actress Sharon Tate. Tate, who had been in a half dozen movies, including *The Valley of the Dolls*, and had had a recurring role as bank secretary Janet Trego on *The Beverly Hillbillies*, was renting the house with her husband, the Polish film director and Holocaust survivor Roman Polanski.

Manson went around to the caretaker's house and talked to the property's owner, Rudi Altobelli, who confirmed that Melcher had moved. Altobelli warned Manson not to disturb the new occupants.

When Altobelli and Tate flew to Rome the next day, the actress expressed concern about the creepy-looking guy she had seen prowling around the property.

In June, Family member Charles Watson defrauded a black drug dealer named Bernard Crowe, who threatened to retaliate by wiping out the Family. Manson responded by shooting and wounding Crowe in his Hollywood apartment. When the newspapers reported soon after that a Black Panther had been found dead, Manson wrongly assumed it was Crowe and that the race war was about to begin.

On July 25, 1969, two days after the first moon landing and three weeks before the Woodstock music festival, Manson sent Family lieutenant Bobby Beausoleil to rob and kill a music teacher named Gary Hinman and make it look like a Black Panther hit. Manson himself arrived in the middle of the two-day-long torture session to slice off a piece of Hinman's ear and compel his acolytes to finish the job. One of the participants, probably Susan Atkins, used Hinman's blood to write "Political piggy" and draw a panther paw on a wall.

Watson was arrested on August 6 while driving Hinman's car. Manson declared that Helter Skelter had begun, and on August 8 he dispatched Watson, Atkins, Patricia Krenwinkel, and Linda Kasabian to kill everyone at the Cielo Drive address.

Watson had been to the house at least once before, possibly for a botched drug deal involving Tate's friend, celebrity hairdresser Jay Sebring. Watson climbed a pole and cut the telephone lines, then ordered Kasabian to keep a lookout by the car as he and the two other girls headed toward the house.

The first victim was Steven Parent, an eighteen-year-old friend of caretaker William Garretson, whom Watson shot as the boy was pulling out of the driveway. Watson and the two girls then broke into the main house through a window screen and butchered Sebring, Polanski's screenwriter friend Wojciech Frykowski, coffee heiress Abigail Folger, and Tate, who was eight and a half months pregnant. (Polanski himself was working in London, where Tate had visited him just three weeks earlier.) Again, on orders to do "something witchy," the murderers left a message: the word "piggy," written in Tate's blood on the front door.

After the killers told Manson what they had done, he went to the house to wipe away fingerprints.

On August 10, Manson drove with the same four assailants, as well as Leslie Van Houten and Clem Grogan, to the randomly chosen home of supermarket executive Leno LaBianca in the Los Feliz neighborhood. Manson broke into the house, awakened LaBianca and his wife, Rosemary, and ordered Watson, Krenwinkel, and Van Houten to kill them in the most dramatic fashion.

Once again, Manson was not present for any of the actual murders—he had given the orders, then left. He was driving Kasabian, Atkins, and Grogan to Venice Beach, where he ordered them to kill an actor of Kasabian's acquaintance, Saladin Nader. (As Manson drove away, the conscience-stricken young woman deliberately knocked at the wrong door.)

In the wake of the grisly killings, wealthy Angelenos beefed up their security or left town altogether, fearing that the unsolved spree wasn't over.

Over the next few weeks, another Family member was arrested in connection with the Hinman case and Manson himself was arrested for stealing Volkswagens to use as dune buggies. As investigators from several different jurisdictions compared evidence, the three sets of torture killings were eventually connected—and the trial of the century was set to begin.

Susan Atkins bragged to a cellmate that there was a hit list of additional targets, including actors Richard Burton and Elizabeth Taylor. Singer Tom Jones would be forced to have sex with Atkins before his throat was cut. Frank Sinatra was going to be skinned alive while listening to his own music.

With Kasabian as the star witness for the prosecution, Manson, Watson, Atkins, Krenwinkel, and Van Houten were convicted for their roles in the Tate/LaBianca murders. And two of Manson's wishes came true: he was returned to the penal system that he never wanted to leave; and through bootleg recordings and cover versions, his music has become available to listeners around the world. ★

29

SAL MINEO

Was the Switchblade Kid as confused as his rebel role model?

a troubled sidekick, forever stuck in the shadow of James Dean? Hardly. Sal Mineo earned as many Oscar nominations as his idol and lived long enough to make peace with himself. His tragic death was not as scandalous as many believed at the time.

Salvatore Mineo Jr. was born in 1939 in East Harlem and raised in the Bronx, where kids teased him for being the son of a Sicilian casket maker. To compensate, he ingratiated himself with the local gangs. But young Sal wasn't a bad seed. He was a soft-hearted kid who liked movies.

Mineo's mother signed him up for acting and dance lessons. Soon he landed a role on Broadway, in Tennessee Williams' play *The Rose Tattoo*. Sal had one line—"The goat is in the yard"—for which he was paid $65 a week. When the play left New York for a run in Chicago, Mineo went with it, leaving home for the first time. On the train west, the crying boy was comforted by Williams himself.

Another imposing adult who mentored the young actor was Yul Brynner. At thirteen, Mineo was cast in the Broadway production of *The King and I*. After he worked up the nerve to ask the star for makeup tips, Brynner befriended him and gave him acting advice that Mineo would take to Hollywood.

With a few TV dramas under his belt, he was cast as a hoodlum in the film *Six Bridges to Cross* (1955), beating out a contender named Clint

Sal Mineo during the filming of *Exodus*, 1960. *Time & Life Pictures/Getty Images*

Eastwood. In the same year Mineo worked with Charlton Heston in *The Private War of Major Benson*. But it was *Rebel Without a Cause* that changed his career and his life. Mineo was cast as Plato, a rich teen with father issues who, in the course of one fateful day, forms a surrogate family with classmates played by James Dean and Natalie Wood. Dean, whose sexuality has long been the subject of gossip and guessing games, encouraged Mineo to mine the homosexual subtext of his role.

Unlike Dean, Mineo earned an Academy Award nomination, for Best Supporting Actor. He was the second youngest actor ever nominated, after Brandon DeWilde for 1953's *Shane*, yet it was Dean who became a legend. On September 30, 1955, James Dean was killed in a car accident—just weeks before *Rebel* was released. He and Mineo had just completed production on the Western *Giant* and were slated to work together again on the boxing movie *Somebody Up There Likes Me*. Instead, Mineo was paired with newcomer Paul Newman.

> "Diminutive and sad-eyed, his performance perfectly captured the film's themes of youthful desperation, and struck a chord with audiences as well as critics."
>
> — *The New York Times, on Sal Mineo's performance in Rebel Without a Cause*

In the late 1950s, Mineo was nicknamed the "Switchblade Kid" for his tendency to play troubled delinquents. Yet he also released two pop records that landed on the charts and conspicuously dated several starlets. Chief among them was Jill Haworth, his fifteen-year-old co-star in *Exodus*, director Otto Preminger's 1960 founding-of-Israel epic, for which Mineo earned his second nomination as Best Supporting Actor. Haworth moved into his house in Beverly Hills. But Mineo couldn't continue the charade, and the relationship was short-lived.

As starring opportunities began to dry up and Mineo started accepting supporting and small-screen roles, he also grew to come to terms with his sexuality. In 1969, Mineo bought the rights to a prison play called *Fortune and Men's Eyes*, which featured an explicit gay-rape scene. Mineo directed the play and cast a young Don Johnson as his co-star. Although the play did well in Los Angeles, it stalled on Broadway. Mineo nonetheless continued to focus on theater, taking TV roles to stave off bankruptcy. He played a bisexual burglar in the successful 1976 play *P.S. Your Cat Is Dead*, by James Kirkwood Jr.

Mineo was excited about his next project, a conspiracy thriller about the assassination of Robert F. Kennedy to be called *Sirhan Sirhan*. It wasn't to be. On February 12, 1976, as Mineo was walking home after a play rehearsal, he was knifed in the alley behind his West Hollywood apartment.

Detectives initially focused their investigation on Mineo's friends and acquaintances, thinking that the murder might have resulted from a sexual liaison gone wrong. John Lennon offered a reward for the capture of the killer. While mourners such as Natalie Wood, Dennis Hopper, Desi Arnaz Jr., and *Rebel* director Nicholas Ray gathered for the New York funeral, L.A. police searched Mineo's apartment and found gay pornography. A broader investigation was shuttered due to lack of evidence.

Sixteen months later, a woman named Theresa Williams told police that her pizza-deliveryman husband, Lionel, had come home that night with his shirt soaked in blood and announced that he had killed Sal Mineo. Cops interviewed Lionel Williams inside the Los Angeles County Jail, where he was serving time on a bad check charge. He said he was anxious to talk about the murder, but then claimed he'd heard that Mexican gang members had killed Mineo over a botched drug deal. A few months later, after Williams was jailed on fraud charges in Michigan, he boasted to his cellmates about killing Mineo, saying that it was a random robbery gone wrong.

Williams was extradited to California and convicted of Mineo's murder in 1979. He was released after twelve years in prison. Despite the conviction, the myth persists that the Switchblade Kid was looking for trouble. ★

30

JEAN SEBERG

Did the FBI drive the politicized pixie to suicide?

*J*ean Seberg was never a big Hollywood star. Over a twenty-year career she made thirty-seven movies, many of them in Europe. In France she was a fashion icon of the 1960s. But in her home country, the government regarded the little-known actress as an enemy and plotted to destroy her.

Jean Seberg was born in Marshalltown, Iowa, in 1938. At age seventeen, the fresh-faced farm girl won a nationwide talent search to star in Otto Preminger's religious epic *Saint Joan* (1957). Although Preminger's retelling of the Joan of Arc legend was based on a play by George Bernard Shaw, was adapted by Graham Greene, and costarred legend John Gielgud, it was a huge flop. After the bad reviews, the defiant director cast Seberg as another French girl in his next movie, an adaptation of the bestselling coming-of-age memoir *Bonjour Tristesse* (1958). That movie, which co-starred David Niven and Deborah Kerr, was another box-office disappointment.

Nevertheless, the film got Seberg noticed in France, where avant-garde director Jean-Luc Godard cast her in his groundbreaking movie *Breathless* in 1960. In the signature film of the French New Wave, Seberg played the innocent American girlfriend of a thief played by Jean-Paul Belmondo. Belmondo was the quintessence of cool, yet it was Seberg who became a trendsetter. Beatnik chicks on both sides of the Atlantic emulated her

Seberg won the lead role in *Saint Joan* over 18,000 contestants in a nationwide talent contest. Despite negative reviews for her performance, she quickly became a style icon. *AFP/Getty Images*

on- and off-screen look: short pixie haircut, boat-neck T-shirt, tight black slacks, and flat-heeled slippers.

After a two-year marriage to French director François Moreuil, Seberg returned to Hollywood, where she was cast as a woman on the verge of a breakdown in *Lilith* (1964) opposite Warren Beatty, and as a muse to poet Sean Connery in *A Fine Madness* (1966). In real life she played muse to Romain Gary, a Russian-born French diplomat, novelist, and director whom she wed in 1962. Together they had a son named Diego. As she struggled through a turbulent marriage, Seberg paid the bills with roles in the Hollywood musical *Paint Your Wagon* and the disaster movie *Airport* in 1969 and 1970, respectively.

While the couple was separated in 1970, Seberg became pregnant again. Gary said the child was his, but Seberg later stated that the father was a student named Carlos Navarra. The FBI spread a third story: the father was Raymond Hewitt, of the revolutionary leftist group the Black Panthers.

Like many celebrities of the Vietnam era, Seberg supported liberal causes, and she became more outspoken after the assassinations of Martin Luther King Jr. and Robert F. Kennedy. Documents uncovered by a Congressional committee and made public in 1982 show that FBI director J. Edgar Hoover wanted Seberg "neutralized." An FBI agent named Richard Held proposed sending a tip to a Hollywood gossip columnist claiming that the unborn child was a proto-Panther. In files released under the Freedom of Information Act, Held wrote to Hoover: "The possible publication of Seberg's plight could cause her embarrassment and serve to cheapen her image with the general public."

Given the go-ahead, Held sent a pseudonymous letter to *Los Angeles Times* columnist Joyce Haber, who wrote an item indicating that a certain married movie star had been impregnated by a black terrorist. The item was subsequently reprinted by other publications, including *Newsweek*, which explicitly identified the actress as Seberg. Within days of reading the *Newsweek* article, Seberg miscarried, two months premature.

Seberg called a press conference in Marshalltown, where reporters could see that the stillborn baby girl in the open coffin was white. She received a public apology and a token payment from the publications that had printed the gossip, but the damage was done. Although she subsequently married filmmaker Dennis Berry (and may have also married Algerian playboy Ahmed Hasni in an unofficial ceremony), Seberg remained distraught. She was certain that the FBI was tapping her phone and bugging her apartment, and every year on the anniversary of the miscarriage, she attempted suicide.

Seberg died in August 1979 at the age of forty. Her body was discovered in the back seat of her car in a Paris suburb, two weeks after she had been reported missing. The disputed verdict was that she overdosed on barbiturates and alcohol. Seberg was buried not in Marshalltown, where she had predicted Hollywood would discard her as a has-been country bumpkin, but in Paris, where her funeral was attended by the great intellectuals of the era. ★

JAYNE MANSFIELD

Was the blonde bombshell brainless?

*J*t got overlooked because of her other attributes, but sex symbol Jayne Mansfield had a good head on her shoulders. And she didn't lose it in a car accident.

When Jayne Mansfield burst onto the screen in 1956's *The Girl Can't Help It*, the blonde bombshell seemed to be poured from the same mold as Marilyn Monroe. The girl born Vera Jayne Palmer in 1933 couldn't help that she was a smart cookie playing dumb.

Raised in Dallas and trained to play violin and piano, the beauty queen with the genius IQ got pregnant and married a boy named Paul Mansfield while she was still in high school. While studying at the University of Texas and Southern Methodist University, Jayne literally carried her infant daughter to class. In 1953, the young family moved to California, where Jayne enrolled in drama classes at UCLA.

Mansfield spoke five languages and was conversant in philosophy, but it was the eye-popping measurements she listed as 40"-21"-35" that paid the bills. She dyed her dark tresses blonde, did cheesecake modeling assignments, and caught the attention of Hollywood. After a few small movie roles and a divorce, Mansfield moved to New York and starred in the 1955 Broadway production of *Will Success Spoil Rock Hunter?* The comedy, with Mansfield playing a Monroe-like movie star who flirts with an ad executive, ran for more than 400 performances.

Hollywood was now salivating for the new sensation. Before reprising her Broadway role on the big screen, she starred in 1956's *The Girl Can't Help It*, a rock 'n' roll romp that played up the dumb-blonde stereotype that had stifled Monroe. Although Mansfield, Monroe, and Mamie Van Doren were playing the same game, Mansfield played it with particular zeal, stealing the spotlight at publicity events like the 1957 dinner where she upstaged Sophia Loren. (The famous photo of Loren eyeing Mansfield's cleavage is now a popular postcard.) Like Monroe, Mansfield also wanted a serious acting career. In 1957, she starred in the drama *The Wayward Bus*, based on a novel by John Steinbeck, which resembled Monroe's 1956 drama *Bus Stop*. (Mansfield would later act in *Bus Stop* on stage.)

In 1958, Mansfield married Hungarian bodybuilder Mickey Hargitay. The newlyweds moved into a pink palace on Sunset Boulevard with twenty bedrooms and thirteen bathrooms, and soon they started a family. Mansfield and Hargitay had three children, including daughter Mariska (who would eventually star in the TV series *Law and Order: Special Victims Unit*).

In 1963, a year after Monroe's tragic death, Jayne Mansfield became the first mainstream movie star to do a nude scene, in the comedy *Promises! Promises!* Subsequently her marriage broke up, and in the last four years of her life she was reduced to doing TV appearances, European sex comedies, and publicity ploys. Those gambits included an album of classical poetry readings, songs with a young guitarist named Jimi Hendrix, and photos with a well-known Satanist—which fed the eventual legend that her death was the result of a curse. By 1967, Mansfield had married for the third time and borne her fifth child. She soon became estranged from her husband, Italian film director Matt Cimber.

Jayne Mansfield is believed to have had an IQ of 163—about the same as Mozart, Darwin, and Ben Franklin. *Michael Ochs Archives/ Getty Images*

On the night of June 28, Mansfield was in the midst of a nightclub tour when she and her boyfriend, Sam Brody; four Chihuahuas; three of Mansfield's children; and a young driver left Biloxi, Mississippi, for a show in New Orleans. As they drove along a dark highway, an eighteen-wheeler ahead of them slowed unexpectedly. The convertible containing Mansfield slammed into the back of the big rig.

The bleached-blonde movie star was essentially scalped (but not, contrary to legend, decapitated). Also killed in the accident were the other two adults and a dog. The three children were physically unharmed but undoubtedly scarred for life. Jayne Mansfield was thirty-four years old, younger at the time of her death than Marilyn Monroe had been. ★

32

NATALIE WOOD

What caused the Russian doll to get smashed?

No one has seriously suggested that Natalie Wood was murdered. But her death by drowning at age forty-three was both suspicious and a shame. Wood was arguably the most underrated and influential actress of the post–World War II era.

Natalie Wood was born Natalia Zakharenko to Russian émigré parents in San Francisco in 1938. (The family later changed its name to Gurdin.) Like Elizabeth Taylor, the raven-haired beauty was a child star who grew into a social trendsetter and married the same man twice. It was Wood's second marriage to actor Robert Wagner that would prove fatal.

Young Natalie played a child skeptical of Santa Claus in the 1947 holiday classic *Miracle on 34th Street.* She retained that fierce intelligence and independence as a teenager in the iconic films *Rebel Without a Cause* (1955) and *The Searchers* (1956). During the former film, she surrendered her virginity to middle-aged director Nicholas Ray, dated co-star James Dean, and earned the first of a record three Oscar nominations before age twenty-five.

The rebellious Wood also dated Dennis Hopper and Elvis Presley (whom she later described as a square) before marrying her long-time crush Wagner, nine years her senior, in 1957.

Wood's career stalled until 1961, when she starred in two films, the hit adaptation of the musical *West Side Story* and the obsessive-love story

In 1956, Natalie Wood was a high-school student starring alongside John Wayne in *The Searchers.*
NY Daily News via Getty Images

Splendor in the Grass, for which she earned her second Academy Award nomination. Off screen, Wood and *Splendor* co-star Warren Beatty began an affair that would bring out Wagner's violent jealousy—and not for the last time. Soon after the cuckolded husband stalked his wife and her co-star with a loaded gun, Wood and Wagner divorced.

In the early 1960s, Wood replaced the late Marilyn Monroe as the sexiest star in Hollywood. She played a stripper in the movie musical *Gypsy* in 1962, had pre-marital sex with Steve McQueen in 1963's *Love with the Proper Stranger* (earning her third Oscar nomination), and was a proto-feminist in the comedies *Sex and the Single Girl* (1964) and *The Great Race* (1965). Wood was a Golden Globe nominee for the Southern potboilers *Inside Daisy Clover* (1965) and *This Property Is Condemned* (1966), both of which co-starred her old friend and Van Nuys High School (in Los Angeles) classmate Robert Redford.

Wood turned down the chances to co-star with Redford in *Barefoot in the Park*, with newcomer Dustin Hoffman in *The Graduate*, and with her soon-to-be-ex boyfriend Beatty in *Bonnie and Clyde*. When she returned to acting in 1969 after a three-year mental-health hiatus, she struck gold with the spouse-swapping comedy *Bob & Carol &Ted &Alice*. Wood's contract for a percentage of the box-office receipts earned her a record $3 million.

In 1969, she married British producer Richard Gregson, and a year later she gave birth to their daughter, Natasha. Gregson cheated on Wood, and the couple separated in 1971, after which Wood dated politician Jerry Brown. In 1972, she reconciled with and remarried Wagner, who had built a successful television career on the action series *It Takes a Thief*. The wedding ceremony took place on a boat off the coast of Los Angeles.

Wood and Wagner had a daughter named Courtney in 1974. While raising her two girls, Wood mostly confined her acting to television, including a 1976 TV production of *Cat on a Hot Tin Roof* with Wagner, the 1979 miniseries *From Here to Eternity*, and episodes of Wagner's series *Switch* and *Hart to Hart*. Meanwhile, the plum movie roles for actresses were going to peers such as Jane Fonda and Faye Dunaway.

In 1981, Wood signed to do a science-fiction movie called *Brainstorm* with rising star Christopher Walken. Most of the shoot was in North Carolina, but Wood returned to California in November and invited Walken to spend Thanksgiving weekend with her and Wagner aboard their yacht, *Splendour*, named after one of Wood's most memorable films (albeit with the British spelling).

Wood had always been fearful of water. Her mother claimed that a gypsy had predicted Natalie would drown to death—a prediction that almost came true while the child actress was shooting a scene for the 1949 film *The Green Promise*. During the production of *Splendor in the Grass*, director Elia Kazan had to trick Wood into doing scenes at a reservoir, and for the miniseries *From Here to Eternity* Wood pleaded in vain for a double to do her swimming scenes.

On the night of November 28, 1981, Wood, Wagner, and Walken dined, drank, and caused a commotion at the Harbor Reef restaurant on Catalina Island. After dinner they returned to the boat. In Wagner's 2008 memoir, *Pieces of My Heart: A Life*, he claims that Walken encouraged Wood to spend more time acting and that the two men got into a heated argument about it. Biographers have speculated that the real subject of the argument was an affair between Wood and Walken. More than twenty years after the fact, Wagner admitted that he smashed a wine bottle on a table and that Wood fled below deck.

Wagner says that after midnight he noticed that Wood was not on the boat and that the motorized dinghy (named *Valiant*, after one of his movies) was missing. At 1:30 a.m., he radioed for a boat to take him to the restaurant, but his wife was not there. At 5:30, the Coast Guard found the dinghy in a cove. Two hours later, they found Wood's body in the water, dressed in a nightgown and a down jacket.

Although Wagner initially told the searchers that Wood had been trying to take the dinghy to a restaurant on shore, he later suggested that the dinghy had been banging on the side of the yacht and Wood must have slipped into the water while trying to secure it. The Los Angeles County Coroner declared the death an accidental drowning.

But the captain of the yacht, Dennis Davern, wrote a book called *Goodbye Natalie, Goodbye Splendour* that describes the night differently. He says that Wood and Walken openly flirted in the restaurant and that the argument on the boat turned into a physical fight. Davern identified Wood's body the next morning, and he says it was covered with bruises.

Wood's younger sister, actress Lana Wood, insists that the aquaphobic Natalie would not have entered or even handled the dinghy in dark waters without urgent necessity. Because suspicions persists that she was pushed or died trying to escape an attacker, both Dennis Davern and Lana Wood have called for the case to be reopened.

Natalie Wood's grave in Los Angeles' Westwood Village Memorial Park now rivals Marilyn Monroe's as the most visited in the cemetery. The posthumous interest in Wood is shared by the Los Angeles County Sheriff's Department. As this book was going to press, the department reopened its investigation into her death. ★

33

JOHN BELUSHI

Did a cursed screenplay kill the comic heavyweight?

*J*ohn Belushi belongs to the 1970s the way James Dean belongs to the 1950s. The collision that killed the star of *Animal House* was between a man and his appetites. It seems unlikely that Belushi would have had a long life, even if he hadn't read the supposedly cursed script that has been blamed for the deaths of several stars.

Officially, Belushi died at age thirty-three from an intravenous overdose of cocaine and heroin at the Chateau Marmont hotel in Los Angeles. But another theory is that he succumbed to a screenplay called *Atuk* that later killed Sam Kinison, John Candy, and Chris Farley.

In the 1970s, Belushi was riding high. Literally. After starring in stage productions for the improvisation troupe Second City in his native Chicago and in the off-Broadway *National Lampoon Lemmings* in New York, the hyperactive heavyweight became a sensation as part of the new sketch-comedy show *Saturday Night Live*, alongside Bill Murray, Chevy Chase, Gilda Radner, and other comedy stars.

In the Studio 54 era, fame and drugs danced hand in hand, and cocaine fueled Belushi's brand of kamikaze comedy. It also powered his burgeoning movie career. In the 1978 frat-house comedy *Animal House*, he only had fifteen lines of dialogue, but his maniacal eyebrows said plenty. Cocaine was rampant on the set of *The Blues Brothers*, a 1980 musical spin-off of an *SNL* routine with Belushi's cohort Dan Aykroyd, where everyone agreed it

Two years before his death, John Belushi starred as "Joliet" Jake Blues in *The Blues Brothers*, based on a popular *Saturday Night Live* skit. *Photograph by Chris Walter. WireImage/ Getty Images*

would be hilarious to destroy seventy-six cop cars (a record for automotive carnage that would be broken by the movie's 2000 sequel).

When Belushi got too big for *SNL*, the 222-pound star began accumulating half-baked movie ideas, scripts for which lay piled on his coffee table. Among them was an adaptation of a 1963 Canadian novel called *The Incomparable Atuk* by Mordecai Richler. It told the story of a poetic Eskimo (now more properly called an Inuit) who leaves the Arctic for Toronto. In the script by Tod Carroll, shortened to the title *Atuk*, the innocent Inuit follows a documentary crew to Manhattan, where classic fish-out-of-water shenanigans ensue.

Belushi had supposedly expressed interest in the project before he went on his final bender. On the last night of his life, March 4, 1982, he drank heavily at a celebrity hideout called On The Rocks, above the Sunset Strip nightclub The Roxy. After the bar closed, he was dragged back to bungalow #3 at the Chateau Marmont by a drug dealer named Cathy Evelyn Smith. (Smith, a groupie who was the inspiration for Gordon Lightfoot's song "Sundown," had first met Belushi in 1976 and had reconnected with him in Los Angeles through her drug clients Keith Richards and Ron Wood of The Rolling Stones.)

Around 3 a.m., Belushi and Smith were briefly visited by Robin Williams and Robert De Niro. Williams later told Bob Woodward for the book *Wired: The Short Life and Fast Times of John Belushi* (1984) that they were appalled to see Smith giving Belushi heroin, a drug to which the comedy star wasn't accustomed. The visitors quickly left.

When Belushi took a shower at approximately 9 a.m., Smith borrowed his Mercedes to get some food. Around noon, Belushi was discovered dead in bed by his personal trainer, martial artist Bill "Superfoot" Wallace.

A few weeks after Belushi's funeral on Martha's Vineyard, Massachusetts, where a leather-clad Aykroyd led a parade of Harley-Davidson motorcycles and played a tape of The Ventures' fuzz-guitar song "The 2000 Pound Bee" per Belushi's request, Smith confessed to a tabloid that she had administered the drugs. Eventually she was extradited from Canada and served fifteen months in prison.

In 1988, the *Atuk* screenplay found its way to another comedic cannonball, stand-up comedian Sam Kinison, who agreed to star. But after one day of shooting in New York, Kinison insisted the script was no good and quit. He was successfully sued by the producers and thus was destitute when he died in a car crash in 1992.

The next to inherit the script was John Candy, an alumnus of *SCTV*, the Canadian sketch-comedy show on which Belushi was scheduled to make an appearance the week he died. Candy was in the midst of reading the *Atuk* screenplay when he succumbed to a fatal heart attack in 1994, the day before the twelfth anniversary of Belushi's death.

SNL veteran Chris Farley, whose idol was Belushi, read the script in 1997 and was enthusiastic about making the movie. Soon after, he died of a cocaine overdose at thirty-three (the same age as Belushi). The heartless hooker with whom Farley had been smoking crack in his apartment in Chicago's John Hancock Tower took pictures of his bloated, lifeless body before she left.

(Myth-mongers also point out that Farley had shown the script to his *SNL* colleague Phil Hartman, who considered playing a supporting role in the film. Six months after Farley died, Hartman was fatally shot by his wife in a murder-suicide.)

Whether there is an actual curse attached to the *Atuk* screenplay is a question for a higher authority. But consider that all the men mentioned as potential stars of the film were dangerously overweight, and all but Candy were hardcore drug abusers. (Thus a similar "curse" has been attributed to the stillborn script for *A Confederacy of Dunces*, based on the posthumous 1980 novel by John Kennedy Toole about an obese curmudgeon. Belushi, Candy, and Farley were all considered for the lead role—but so was Will Ferrell, who is alive and well.)

Atuk screenwriter Tod Carroll has said that he is not superstitious (even though his first name means "death" in German). His explanation for why certain projects soar while others crash and burn may be contained in the title of his successfully produced follow-up: 1988's *Clean and Sober*. ★

"Following Belushi's career is akin to taking a crash course in modern American comedy."

— *Variety* magazine

34

HEATH LEDGER

What caused the rising star to fall?

eath Ledger wasn't getting high when he died of a drug overdose. He was coming down from a rollercoaster called the Joker. Born in Perth in 1979, an isolated city on the west coast of Australia, Ledger moved to Sydney at age seventeen to audition for film and television roles. There, the surfer and former field-hockey star felt typecast as a hunk, so after a few years he moved to Los Angeles, where he won his breakthrough role as a charming exchange student in the 1999 teen comedy *10 Things I Hate About You*. Subsequent films included the action movies *A Knight's Tale* and *The Four Feathers*.

On the whole, however, Ledger strayed from the starlight path. He accepted a supporting role in the Revolutionary War drama *The Patriot* and an extended cameo as a suicidal prison guard in *Monster's Ball*—both in 2000—which he followed with the violent Australian crime drama *Ned Kelly*.

Arguably no rising star ever took a bigger chance than Ledger did in *Brokeback Mountain* in 2005. Although a few mainstream movies had alluded to homosexuality, from the sympathetic *Sunday Bloody Sunday* (1971) and *The Boys in the Band* (1970) to the soft-focus *Making Love* (1982) and the sensationalized *Cruising* (1980), Ang Lee's adaptation of a 1997 short story by Annie Proulx was billed as Hollywood's first gay love story. The casting was big news. Ledger won the role of Ennis Del Mar, a taciturn Wyoming cowboy who falls in love with a wrangler named Jack Twist, played by Jake Gyllenhaal.

While Gyllenhaal energized the film, Ledger stole it with his painfully internalized performance. Within the stereotype of the strong and silent cowboy, the lock-jawed Ledger found a core of emptiness and self-loathing. It was a performance of profound understatement, for which Ledger was nominated for an Academy Award for Best Actor. The Academy, which is older and more conservative than the filmmaking community at large, gave the award to Philip Seymour Hoffman for his performance in *Capote*. Although Lee won Best Director, Best Picture went to *Crash*. "It didn't surprise me," Ledger told me of the conservative backlash during an interview in 2006. "But it does baffle me that people can express such hatred toward different forms of love. It's a hatred of something in themselves, perhaps."

Ledger, who had fallen in love with Michelle Williams on the set of *Brokeback Mountain*, continued to dig deeper into his own psyche. He played a heroin addict in the Australian indie *Candy* (2006) and channeled James Dean in the Bob Dylan biopic *I'm Not There* (2007), then landed the role that would drive him to his grave: the villainous Joker in *The Dark Knight*.

During production of the superhero sequel, directed by Christopher Nolan, Ledger was obsessed with method-acting authenticity. Even after the cameras stopped rolling, he suffered bouts of severe depression and insomnia that carried over into his next film, the Terry Gilliam fantasy *The Imaginarium of Doctor Parnassus*.

While on break from filming with Gilliam, Ledger returned to the New York apartment he rented after splitting from Williams (who had given birth to their daughter, Matilda Rose, in 2005). On the morning of January 22, 2008, the Academy Award nominations were announced, and it is not unreasonable to suppose that Ledger was awake to find out whether he or his *I'm Not There* co-star Cate Blanchett had made the cut. (Neither received nominations for that film.)

Ledger was last seen alive at around 1 p.m., when a housekeeper used her key to enter the apartment and change a light bulb. The actor was asleep in bed.

About two hours later, a masseuse arrived for an appointment. When Ledger did not answer the door, she contacted the housekeeper to let her in. Neither was able to rouse Ledger from bed, so the masseuse used the speed dial on Ledger's phone to call actress Mary-Kate Olsen, whom Ledger had been dating for a few months. The masseuse called Olsen at least three times before calling paramedics, who eventually arrived with Olsen's private security guards. They pronounced Ledger dead at approximately 2:45 p.m.

Although initial press reports said a rolled-up $20 bill was found at the bedside and hinted that Ledger had died from a recreational drug overdose, the subsequent autopsy found that he in fact died from a lethal combination of legally prescribed sedatives and anti-depressants. No illegal drugs were found in his apartment or his body.

The producers of *The Dark Knight*—which had the buzz of a blockbuster several months before its release—were unsure how to address Ledger's death. A marketing campaign that had focused on the Joker with the tagline "Why so serious?" was replaced with promotional materials that emphasized simple images of a bat-shaped logo.

Despite the abruptness of his death (and the darkness of the Joker), Ledger's family and friends steered the memorials in a celebratory direction. After his burial service in Perth, attendees were encouraged to frolic in the ocean where he surfed as a teenager. Even the grieving Williams joined them.

Ledger's death at twenty-eight left numerous loose ends. The day after he died he was supposed to meet with director Steven Spielberg about a biography of 1960s activist Tom Hayden. Ledger had also wanted to do a movie about doomed folk singer Nick Drake, whose presumed suicide Ledger had imagined in a tribute video.

Most regrettably, Ledger's final film was left unfinished. Hard-luck director Gilliam, who had suffered a similar (if not fatal) disruption to his movie *The Man Who Killed Don Quixote* (which had enough production disasters to merit a making-of documentary called *Lost in La Mancha*), turned for help to one of the actors Ledger had admired most: Johnny Depp. Depp, as well as Ledger's friends Colin Farrell and Jude Law, agreed to play versions of Ledger's shape-shifting character and complete the movie in the late actor's honor.

Exactly one year after he died, Heath Ledger was nominated for an Academy Award as Best Supporting Actor for his explosive performance in *The Dark Knight*. One month later he became the first posthumous honoree in that category.

Matilda Rose will take possession of the Oscar statuette when she turns eighteen in 2023. ★

PART 4

Mythic MOVIES

35

THE GREAT TRAIN ROBBERY

Did Thomas Edison steal the credit?

Contrary to popular belief, *The Great Train Robbery* was not the first movie to tell a story. And Thomas Edison didn't invent motion pictures any more than he invented audio recording.

Just as a French inventor named Édouard-Léon Scott de Martinville recorded "Au Clair de la Lune" in 1860, seventeen years before Edison recorded "Mary Had a Little Lamb," slide projectors called magic lanterns and flicker devices like the spinning zoetrope had existed for decades before Edison patented the kinetograph camera and kinetoscope projector for use in motion pictures.

And it was not Edison but his assistant, William K. L. Dickson, who invented a motor-and-sprockets system for running strips of film through a camera, in 1891. Naturally the boss stole the credit, and Dickson left the company before his invention paid off. The first Edison-branded films, shot at his Black Maria studio in West Orange, New Jersey, were only a few seconds long, like the one that showed employee Fred Ott sneezing. Subsequent Edison films of boxers, cowboys, and scantily clad dancers were viewed on coin-operated contraptions at fairs and arcades.

After the Lumière brothers in France developed a more portable projector, movies became a shared experience, and in 1895, the world's first movie theater opened in Paris. Most of the movies shown in batches there were mundane, minute-long documentaries, but soon magician-turned-filmmaker Georges Méliès introduced elements of fantasy to films, such

as the scene in his fourteen-minute sci-fi adventure *A Trip to the Moon* during which a spaceship runs into the Man in the Moon's eye.

In America, short newsreels quickly lost their novelty, and vaudeville theaters often screened them at the end of the night to clear the audience. So in 1900, Edison hired a projector technician named Edwin S. Porter to direct movies that were long enough to tell stories. Among Porter's first films were a ten-minute *Jack and the Beanstalk* and the brief documentary *Life of an American Fireman*, both in 1902. Porter incorporated cinematic techniques like close-ups and dream sequences. But it was his eleven-minute Western *The Great Train Robbery*, based on an actual heist and a popular stage show, that is widely considered the first film conceived and shot according to the principles of cinema, rather than theater. It used new tricks such as rear-projection to simulate the blurred landscape outside of a moving train, and cross-cutting between simultaneous events.

The Great Train Robbery is an important early film, but it's hardly the first ever made. *Picture Post/ Getty Images*

Filmed in New Jersey, *The Great Train Robbery* wasn't the first film or even the first Western—there had been a one-reeler about the explorer Kit Carson—but it might be considered the first hit movie. Punctuated with a final shocking image of the mustachioed outlaw played by Gilbert "Broncho Billy" Anderson firing his six-gun at the audience, it proved so addictive that storefronts across the country were converted to movie halls. America's first full-time movie-screening venue was a hall in Pittsburgh called The Nickelodeon, a name that became a generic term for this new type of theater, which generally charged five cents for admission.

Edison wanted more than nickels. He regularly sued his competitors for patent infringement and eventually coerced the major New York producers to join his Motion Picture Patents Company, obliging them to use Edison equipment. Foreign and independently produced films were squeezed out of the market.

One consequence of the Edison monopoly, which the courts ended in 1915, was that aspiring filmmakers fled the reach of his attorneys. They found the perfect hideout in a sunny locale called Hollywood, California. ★

36

THE BIRTH OF A NATION

Was it a cultural milestone—or a racist millstone?

Some scholars say that *The Birth of a Nation* was the greatest achievement of silent cinema. Maybe it's true. But the epic movie might also be Hollywood's greatest shame.

There's no question that D. W. Griffith's film was an unprecedented phenomenon. When it was released in 1915, it was the longest movie in the history of the new medium (three hours and ten minutes, in an era when movies rarely topped one hour) and the most profitable (earning $10 million, the equivalent of more than $200 million today—a mark that wasn't matched until *Snow White and the Seven Dwarfs* more than twenty years later). It set new standards for movie music, as prints arrived at theaters with full-length scores to be played by local orchestras. And most important, it introduced techniques such as close-ups, camera movement, mood lighting, flashbacks, and parallel editing that distinguished cinema from theater and established film as a completely new art form.

That's well and good, but have you ever actually seen the thing? Notwithstanding the historical significance of *The Birth of a Nation*, the film is an abomination. Plenty of scholars and film critics still apologize for *The Birth of a Nation* because, like Leni Riefenstahl's Nazi propaganda film *Triumph of the Will*, it is an important cultural relic from another era. In Griffith's era, white Anglo-Saxon Protestants controlled the history books.

The particular book on which the movie is based was *The Clansman*, a 1905 novel by Thomas Dixon Jr. The book is a potboiler about two families in Civil War–era America, the pro-Union, Northern Stonemans and the pro-Confederacy Camerons. While the families are commingling on the Camerons' South Carolina plantation (and the young'uns are falling in love), war breaks out and the clans choose sides. By the time the smoke clears, President Lincoln is dead and the defeated South is handed over to the carpetbaggers, represented by the Stonemans, and to the freed slaves, represented by white actors in blackface.

The film's racism is overt. All the black characters who are not submissively loyal to their former masters are rapists and/or shiftless drunks. When, during the portion of the film that covers Reconstruction, African-Americans win the right to vote, they stuff the ballot boxes to elect their illiterate kin to state office, where they can pass laws legalizing interracial marriage. Riding to the rescue is the Ku Klux Klan—portrayed here as white-robed avengers on hooded horses who thwart the lascivious former slaves and make sure they don't vote in the next election.

Director David Wark (D. W.) Griffith was the son of a Confederate colonel and was raised in Kentucky. As a young man, he moved to New York and eventually directed 400 short movies for the Biograph Company, but he never forgot his past. He claimed that *The Birth of a Nation*, originally titled *The Clansman*, was true to his experiences growing up in the Reconstruction South.

Griffith and Dixon previewed the movie for the novelist's old classmate from Johns Hopkins University, President Woodrow Wilson. Wilson watched it in the White House with members of

> *"The Birth of a Nation is not a bad film because it argues for evil. Like Riefenstahl's The Triumph of the Will, it is a great film that argues for evil. To understand how it does so is to learn a great deal about film, and even something about evil."*
>
> — Roger Ebert

his cabinet and the Supreme Court and has been widely quoted as saying the film was "like history written with lightning." According to some accounts he added, "My only regret is that it is all so true." But while Mrs. Dixon claimed that the quotes were from a lost letter that the President wrote to her husband, it is more likely that they were cooked up by the film's producers, who hinted at a federal endorsement in coyly worded ads. According to White House documents, Wilson's actual words on the subject were that *The Birth of a Nation* was "an unfortunate production."

As soon as the movie premiered, it ignited fiery protests in black communities. In some white ones, it led to a resurgence of the KKK.

At the behest of the fledgling NAACP (founded in 1909), *The Birth of a Nation* was banned in such cities as Chicago, St. Louis, and Pittsburgh, and it was edited before it could be shown in Boston. Yet wherever the movie was screened, there were audiences willing to pay the exorbitant $2 ticket price. A Massachusetts impresario named Louis B. Mayer made so much money by distributing *The Birth of a Nation* in New England that he was able to start his own movie studio—eventually called Metro-Goldwyn-Mayer.

Griffith was stung by the backlash, and he sunk some of his profits into making the religious epic *Intolerance* (1916). Subsequent rereleases of *The Birth of a Nation* included title-card pleas for peace and freedom of expression.

Yet as the years have passed, evidence of the filmmaker's insensitivity has become hard to ignore. In 1999, the Director's Guild of America changed the name of its highest honor from the D.W. Griffith Award—the award's name since its inception in 1953—to the DGA Lifetime Achievement Award. ★

The Birth of a Nation may have been groundbreaking cinematically, but its glorification of the Ku Klux Klan led to protests, denials of racism from director D. W. Griffith, and a hotly contested legacy even a century later. *Hulton Archive/Getty Images*

37

THE JAZZ SINGER

Was the Al Jolson musical really the first "talkie"?

The 1927 film *The Jazz Singer* was not the first movie with sound. Despite an ad campaign that promised "All talking! All singing!" it was really a silent movie with a few musical interludes and a bit of recorded dialogue.

By then, filmmakers had been tinkering with sound for more than thirty years. Circa 1895, Thomas Edison's assistant William K. L. Dickson made a seventeen-second movie of two male colleagues dancing while Dickson played a jig on a violin. The music was recorded to a separate cylinder. At the time, there was no practical means of synchronizing the two mediums, so the Edison Company concentrated on producing silent movies to accompany arcade machines while sound and projection technology were refined in Europe.

Audiences heard sound with moving images as early as the Paris Exposition of 1900, when patrons wore earphones to listen to a portion of a filmed opera. But for the next two decades, problems with the synchronization, volume, and fidelity of sound made true "talkies" impractical.

In 1919, American inventor Lee De Forest patented a sound-on-film system that added a strip of optically induced audio next to a strip of images. American movie studios soon began hedging their bets as they invested in both sound-on-film and synchronized-disc systems.

Poster for *The Jazz Singer*, 1927. Redferns/ Getty Images

Warner Bros. Supreme Triumph

AL JOLSON

THE JAZZ SINGER

price 25 cents

Sound-on-disc was added in 1921 to some sequences of D. W. Griffith's silent *Dream Street*. Six years later, the upstart Warner Bros. Pictures used the Vitaphone sound-on-disc system to add music and sound effects to the feature-length *Don Juan*, starring John Barrymore. So you might say that *Don Juan* was the first full-length movie with continual sound. It was accompanied by eight shorts of musical performances and a spoken introduction by William H. Hays, the president (i.e., censor) of the Motion Picture Association of America.

In 1927, audiences in New York were able to both see and hear a short film of Charles Lindbergh embarking on his trans-Atlantic plane flight.

On October 6, 1927, Warner Bros. premiered *The Jazz Singer*, a melodrama about a man who defies his devout Jewish parents to become a music-hall entertainer. Like *Don Juan* and German director F. W. Murnau's *Sunrise*, it was essentially a silent movie with overdubbed music and sound effects played on a Vitaphone disc. But the few minutes of star Al Jolson singing and ad-libbing dialogue ("You ain't heard nothin' yet!") were recorded live on the set and thus support the argument that *The Jazz Singer* was the first talkie. However, it should be noted that earlier that year, Fox had released a two-reel short with synchronized dialogue called *They're Coming to Get Me*. So *The Jazz Singer* was the first *full-length* feature with *some* synchronized dialogue. The transition from silent film to talkie was an evolution, not a revolution. (For the record, the first all-talking feature was Warner Bros.' *Lights of New York* in 1928.)

The Jazz Singer was a hit, not so much because sound was a novelty but because Jolson was already a star through widely available phonograph records. The success of the film encouraged theater chains to equip their auditoriums with the necessary projectors and loudspeakers to play talkies (most of which were distributed in the practical sound-on-film format). It also encouraged movie studios to develop quieter equipment and smaller microphones, so actors could move more naturally around the sets. Within two years, Hollywood studios were no longer releasing all-silent films. (The last was a Hoot Gibson shoot-'em-up called *Points West* in 1929.)

That myth about talkies killing the careers of actors with bad voices? It's amusing in *Singin' in the Rain* and the Oscar-winning pseudo-silent *The Artist*, but it's not entirely true to life. Many of the major silent stars were stage-trained performers with strong voices, and even the unconventional or heavily accented voices of silent performers such as Jean Harlow and Greta Garbo were accepted by audiences—which included a lot of forgiving immigrants—after the transition to talkies. The reason Charlie Chaplin kept making pseudo-silents like *City Lights* and *Modern Times* wasn't because he had a bad voice. He simply preferred the pantomime art form. ★

38

THE WIZARD OF OZ

Are myths about the movie a rainbow of lies?

No movie is more mythic—or the source of more muddled information—than *The Wizard of Oz*.

It's not true that a Munchkin committed suicide on camera. It *is* true that makeup malfunctions hospitalized at least two of the cast members. And it *might be* true that Pink Floyd's album *The Dark Side of the Moon* is synchronized to the movie.

The 1939 film was based on the 1900 novel *The Wonderful Wizard of Oz* by L. Frank Baum. Baum was a playwright and newspaper publisher who spent much of his adult life in the Midwest. (For his newspaper in Aberdeen, South Dakota, he wrote editorials decrying the treatment of Native Americans yet urging that they be "exterminated" to put them out of their misery.) When Baum and illustrator W. W. Denslow created the first of more than a dozen *Oz* books, Baum was living in Chicago, where he published a magazine about department-store window displays. He would later say that the name *Oz* was derived from the letters on an alphabetized file cabinet in his office: O–Z.

The Wonderful Wizard of Oz, in which a girl from Kansas is swept up by a cyclone and lands in the magical land of Oz, was a huge hit. Baum and Denslow collaborated on a stage musical, which toured the country for almost a decade, and sold the book to Hollywood, where it was made into

a silent film in 1910. In 1938, MGM planned a sound-and-color version of the beloved book in an attempt to replicate the success of Walt Disney's *Snow White and the Seven Dwarfs* in 1937.

The casting of *The Wizard of Oz* proved problematic. Shirley Temple, whose film career was peaking at the ripe old age of ten, was offered the role of Dorothy, but Fox studio chief Darryl F. Zanuck did not want to lend her to a rival company. So the lead role was assigned to MGM's musical ingénue Judy Garland.

Minnesota-born Garland, whom studio chief Louis B. Mayer ridiculed as his "little hunchback," was a natural trouper from a family of vaudevillians. Though she was just sixteen when she filmed *The Wizard of Oz*, the studio supplied her with amphetamines to meet the grueling production schedule. (She would remain addicted to pills for their rest of her abbreviated life.)

Comedian W. C. Fields was the first choice to play the title character, but MGM balked at his asking price of $100,000 and gave the role instead to contract player Frank Morgan. Accomplished dancer Buddy Ebsen (the future star of *The Beverly Hillbillies* on TV) was originally cast as the Scarecrow, but he was asked to swap roles by Ray Bolger, who had been cast as the Tin Man. After Ebsen agreed, he developed an allergic reaction to the aluminum powder in the Tin Man makeup and was forced to leave the production. He was replaced by Jack Haley, who used a different type of makeup.

Academy Award–winner Gale Sondergaard did makeup and wardrobe tests as the Wicked Witch of the West, but when the role was changed from a slinky temptress to an old hag, Sondergaard bowed out. The role went to Margaret Hamilton. During filming of a scene when the witch leaves Munchkinland in a puff of smoke, Hamilton's green makeup caught on fire, requiring the actress to recuperate for six weeks from burns to her face and hand.

Contrary to urban legend, none of the Munchkins were killed or committed suicide during production. The fluttering object in the background when Dorothy, the Scarecrow, and the Tin Man dance down the Yellow Brick Road toward Oz was not a body but a large bird, one of several that had been added to the setting to make it seem more exotic. Think about it: is it possible that an entire cast and crew would overlook—or incorporate—a hanging body in a scene for a hugely important movie? Besides, the Munchkins had not yet been hired at the time that scene was filmed.

From left, Jack Haley, Bert Lahr, Judy Garland, and Ray Bolger, trying to get past Frank Morgan into the Emerald City. *Moviepix/ Getty Images*

When the Munchkins did arrive at MGM (from Europe), there's little evidence, despite subsequent allegations, that they ran riot through the studio, though they had every reason to be grumpy. Billed collectively as the Singer Midgets, the 122 little people were paid $50 per week—$75 less than Terri, the Cairn Terrier who played Dorothy's dog, Toto.

The production employed fourteen writers and five directors. A preliminary version ran two hours long. After a sneak preview, the studio cut twenty minutes, including a musical number called "The Jitterbug." The song "Somewhere Over the Rainbow" was also on the chopping block until composers E. Y. Harburg and Harold Arlen successfully pleaded with Mayer to keep it in.

The finished product was credited to director Victor Fleming, who also directed *Gone with the Wind* that same year. But whereas *Gone with the Wind* was an immediate sensation, the 1939 release of *Oz* did not recoup the studio's huge investment.

As would later happen to *It's a Wonderful Life*, television turned *The Wizard of Oz* into a beloved classic. It first aired, on CBS, in 1956. Although most people did not have color televisions that would allow them to fully appreciate the Oz sequences, forty-five million viewers tuned in. The annual broadcast was a Christmas-season tradition until 1967, after which it rotated through various holidays and networks for another thirty years. Between theater screenings, television, and home video, *The Wizard of Oz* is believed to be the most watched film in history.

Among those who have undoubtedly watched the film are members of the British art-rock band Pink Floyd. During the 1990s, Internet chat room visitors debated the possibility that the band's 1973 album *The Dark Side of the Moon* corresponded to scenes from *The Wizard of Oz*. There are undeniable similarities between the two works. The cover illustration of the album features a rainbow. One of the posters included with the vinyl edition depicts the Great Pyramids as an Emerald City. And, if the listener syncs the start of the album with the third roar of the MGM lion, there are dozens of uncanny

Neither Ray Bolger nor Judy Garland was the original choice to play the role each immortalized. *MGM Studios/Handout/ Getty Images*

musical correspondences, including the wailing vocal when Dorothy is swept up into the tornado, the heartbeat when she listens to the Tin Man's chest, and a song called "Brain Damage" when the scarecrow laments his empty noggin. Perhaps most notably, the first side of the vinyl album is exactly the same length as the black-and-white portion of the movie.

Members of Pink Floyd have publicly scoffed at the idea, noting that videotape copies of the film were not available for study when the album was recorded. Yet a tech-savvy and well-heeled rock band could easily have obtained a film print to approximate the timing. Obviously it would spoil the fun if the band were to admit that the rumor is true, just as the Beatles always denied that several of their albums contained hints that the real Paul McCartney had been killed in a car accident.

If you want to test it out yourself, there's no place like home. ★

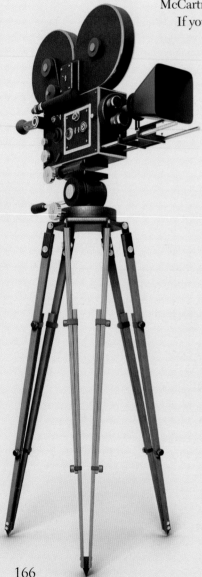

GONE WITH THE WIND

Does the box-office behemoth still blow away the competition?

*I*s *Avatar* the biggest movie of all time? No, that's just an illusion. *Titanic*? Sorry, that ship has sailed.

Your mother should know: the biggest movie of all time is still *Gone with the Wind*, more than seven decades after it first took America by storm.

Entertainment reporters write a lot of stories about box-office totals, and it seems that every week there's a new record of some sort: biggest non-holiday opening for an R-rated comedy, highest per-screen average for an animated sequel, and so on. But these stories are comparing apples to rotten tomatoes. Ticket prices are always rising, and these days there is a surcharge for 3D and IMAX presentations. Comparing films from different eras requires computation and trickery, and it's easier to just declare the latest release a record-breaking hit.

Look at the all-time U.S. box-office chart, and you'll see titles like *Transformers* and *Twilight* but almost nothing that pre-dates the multiplex era. Was an abomination like *You Don't Mess with the Zohan* really a bigger hit than *The Ten Commandments*? Hardly.

The true measure of a film's success is its box-office total adjusted for inflation, reflecting the actual number of tickets sold. On the inflation-adjusted list at boxofficemojo.com, *Gone with the Wind* is victorious, with a domestic gross of more than $1.5 billion, ahead of *Star Wars, The Sound*

of Music, *E.T.*, and (yes) *Titanic*. Its worldwide total is double that amount.

Gone with the Wind was released in 1939, the zenith of Hollywood's golden age. The well-oiled studio machine produced 761 movies that year, including classics such as *The Wizard of Oz*, *Stagecoach*, *Mr. Smith Goes to Washington*, *Wuthering Heights*, *Of Mice and Men*, and *Goodbye, Mr. Chips*. Yet none of them could compete with *Gone with the Wind*, which easily beat the box-office totals of previous blockbusters like *Snow White and the Seven Dwarfs* and remained in theaters throughout the war years. In those days, Hollywood had a virtual monopoly on entertainment expenditures. The studios had a movie theater in every neighborhood and a cozy

> "For almost four hours the drama keeps audiences on the edge of their seats."
>
> — *Time magazine, December 25, 1939, on Gone with the Wind*

relationship with the press. By the time *Gone with the Wind* was released, Hollywood's publicity apparatus ensured that the title was already a household name.

The Margaret Mitchell novel on which the film was based had been published in 1936, and thanks in part to heavy advertising and its validation by the Book-of-the-Month Club, it sold a million copies within six months, at an unprecedented $3 apiece. In 1937, *Gone with the Wind* was awarded the Pulitzer Prize for fiction. A month after the book came out, independent producer David O. Selznick bought the film rights for $50,000, the most ever paid for a debut novel. For the next three years, the casting and production of the film would be front-page news.

The delay was partially a result of Selznick's long struggle to hire superstar Clark Gable as the male lead. Gable was reluctant to do a period piece and didn't think he could live up to the hype. To get him, Selznick contributed $50,000 toward Gable's divorce from Maria Franklin and made a costly distribution deal with Gable's employer at MGM, Louis B. Mayer—who just happened to be Selznick's father-in-law. Then Selznick had to wait for a distribution deal with United Artists to expire. Selznick shrewdly used the time to build publicity for the upcoming film. For the coveted role of Southern belle Scarlett O'Hara, he sponsored a nationwide, closely followed talent search in which 1,400 aspiring actresses were interviewed.

Scores of Hollywood actresses were also seriously considered, from silent star Clara Bow to queen bee Bette Davis to newcomer Lucille Ball. The two finalists who screen tested in Technicolor were *Modern Times* star Paulette Goddard and a little-known English actress named Vivien Leigh. Selznick decided against Goddard because there was controversy over whether she was legally married to Charlie Chaplin. He then concocted a fake story that he had discovered Leigh when she visited the studio with her fiancé, Laurence Olivier. (In reality, Leigh's agent was Selznick's brother.)

Clark Gable and Vivien Leigh as Rhett Butler and Scarlett O'Hara. Gable only agreed to do the film after being offered a $50,000 bonus, which allowed him to divorce his wife and marry actress Carole Lombard. *Photograph by Clarence Sinclair Bull. Getty Images*

After a hugely successful sneak preview in Riverside, California, *Gone with the Wind* officially premiered on December 15, 1939, in Margaret Mitchell's hometown of Atlanta. The governor of Georgia declared it a state holiday, and 12,000 fans surrounded the Loew's Grand Theater to see the stars (who had paraded through downtown the day before, drawing a crowd of 300,000). The next week, the movie opened on Broadway. The Manhattan premiere was broadcast to the few hundred wealthy New Yorkers who owned a television.

By the end of the next decade, television and the courts would end the studio monopoly, but not before *Gone with the Wind* had been seen by at least 100 million American moviegoers—at a time when the entire population of the country was 130 million.

With competition from home theaters, video games, and the Internet, will any film ever sell as many tickets as *Gone with the Wind*? Frankly my dear, I don't think so. But as they say in the movies, tomorrow is another day. ★

40

CITIZEN KANE

Was the fabled film the work of a singular genius?

*I*s *Citizen Kane* the greatest film of all time? You'll get no argument here. But does it validate the singular genius of Orson Welles as the writer, director, and star? No. Although Welles tried to hoard all the credit—and certainly deserves some of it—he was not the film's principle screenwriter.

In 1938, Welles's radio version of *The War of the Worlds* caused a sensation (although reports of widespread panic are overstated, since the broadcast was clearly identified as a production of the Mercury Theatre on the Air and not a newscast). The next year, at age twenty-four, Welles was offered an extraordinary contract by RKO Pictures in Hollywood: a two-film deal, with full control over the script, casting, and final edit.

Welles initially planned to do a film version of Joseph Conrad's masterpiece *Heart of Darkness* using a first-person camera technique, but he couldn't trim the budget enough to satisfy the studio. Then he proposed a political thriller called *The Smiler with the Knife*, but RKO didn't like his choice of leading lady, ingénue Lucille Ball.

The studio agreed to his third idea, a fictional biography tentatively titled *John Citizen, USA*. Welles' idea was to depict a multifaceted portrait of a powerful man—someone like Howard Hughes. At the behest of his radio colleague John Houseman, Welles met with Herman Mankiewicz, a

screenwriting veteran who needed a job. Mankiewicz was a former reporter for the *New York Times* who had contributed to such films as *Horse Feathers*, *Monkey Business*, *Dinner at Eight*, and *The Wizard of Oz*, often without credit. Since 1925 he had been toying with a script about newspaper publisher William Randolph Hearst and his actress girlfriend Marion Davies, both of whom the alcoholic writer had known socially until he wore out his welcome. The concept—in particular the method of storytelling, using recollections of the protagonist's colleagues—was similar enough to Welles' that the two agreed to collaborate.

With Welles' lieutenant Houseman cracking the whip, Mankiewicz produced a complete draft of the screenplay, which Welles annotated, streamlined, and shot. In later years, Houseman credited Welles and cinematographer Gregg Toland with the innovative deep-focus visuals but said that Mankiewicz deserved "total" credit for the screenplay, for which the writer was paid $22,833.35. Mankiewicz's family has been more diplomatic. His grandson, film critic Ben Mankiewicz, has said that the script was "95 percent Herman and 5 percent Orson." The younger Mankiewicz notes that his grandfather was privy to a special secret: Hearst dubbed a particular part of Davies' anatomy "Rosebud."

When the movie premiered on May 1, 1941, RKO publicity referred to Welles as "the one-man band, directing, acting, and writing." And Welles himself fought to keep from sharing the spotlight. He had withheld writing credits from others on his radio productions, and he expected the same arrangement in Hollywood. It has been rumored that he offered Mankiewicz an additional $10,000 to keep quiet.

He did not keep quiet. After newspapers hailed *Citizen Kane* as a work of genius, Mankiewicz waged a campaign in the press and filed a grievance with the Writers Guild of America. The writing credit was changed to include both names. Mankiewicz's came first. (Influential film critic Pauline Kael made a persuasive case that under current WGA rules, Welles would not be entitled to any credit at all.)

At the 1942 Academy Award ceremony, *Citizen Kane* won one award, despite being nominated for nine. That award, for Best Original Screenplay, was shared by Welles and Mankiewicz, with the faintest sour note from the "one-man band." ★

"There but for the grace of God, goes God," *Citizen Kane* scriptwriter Herman J. Mankiewicz said of Orson Welles, according to film critic Pauline Kael. *Keystone/Getty Images*

41

CASABLANCA

Did the usual suspects almost sabotage a classic?

*P*olls say it's America's all-time favorite movie, and historians say it's the high point of the studio system, but *Casablanca* was a mess to make.

In 1938, playwright Murray Bennett and his wife visited a bar in the free south of occupied France, where an American jazz pianist entertained a crowd of Frenchmen, Germans, and wartime refugees. Bennett decided that a bar in a neutral zone would be a fertile setting for a romantic drama, and wrote the play *Everybody Comes to Rick's* (with co-author Joan Allison) based on his experience. It was never published and failed to find a Broadway producer.

The play's script did, however, reach the story department of Warner Bros. studios on December 8, 1941—one day after the Japanese attack on Pearl Harbor pulled the United States into World War II. The character arc in the play mirrored the end of American isolationism, and in a patriotic fervor, producer Hal Wallis bought the script for $20,000—an unprecedented sum for an unproduced play.

In January 1942, a Warner Bros. publicist sent an item to *The Hollywood Reporter* announcing that Ronald Reagan and Anne Sheridan would star in the upcoming production, now called *Casablanca*. Yet Wallis was in the midst of leaving Warner Bros. to produce *Casablanca* independently, and he had no intention of casting Reagan, who was due to join the Army soon. For the male lead Rick Blaine, Wallis wanted Humphrey Bogart, who had never been in a romance but was riding high on the success of *The Maltese Falcon*. Wallis resisted pressure to cast George Raft, the Mob-connected actor who desperately wanted the part.

Sheridan remained under consideration for the female lead until the character was changed from an American to a European who was torn between her Czech husband and the Yankee ex-lover who runs a bar in Morocco's largest city. Wallis wanted Swedish actress Ingrid Bergman to play Ilsa Lund, but Bergman was under contract with producer David O. Selznick, so Wallis traded him the rights to Olivia De Havilland for another project. (Until 1943, when De Havilland successfully sued Warner Bros., actors under contract were traded as readily as pro athletes.)

The role of freedom fighter Victor Laszlo went to Austrian émigré Paul Henreid, who insisted on above-the-title billing alongside Bogart (whom he considered a mediocre actor) and Bergman (who considered Henreid a prima donna). The villainous Nazi was a natural fit for Conrad Veidt, the German-born actor who had starred in the silent classics *The Cabinet of Dr. Caligari* (1919) and *The Man Who Laughs* (1928). (The latter role inspired the look of the Joker in the Batman comics.) Wallis considered casting a female singer such as Ella Fitzgerald or Lena Horne as nightclub entertainer Sam before offering the role to Dooley Wilson, a jazz drummer who did not play the piano in real life.

With the notable exceptions of Englishmen Claude Rains and Sydney Greenstreet, almost all of the supporting actors were Europeans who had been personally affected by the upheavals in Europe. (S. Z. "Cuddles" Sakall, who played the waiter Carl, had two sisters who later died in concentration camps.) When the cameras were rolling, there was tremendous conviction in their performances.

But first they had to have something to say. Even during production, the script was continually being revised by four writers who rarely worked in the same room together. Bergman complained that she didn't know which of the two men her character really loved. Director Michael Curtiz assured her that the ambiguity would benefit the film.

It's not true, as has been suggested elsewhere, that there was uncertainty about which man Ilsa would choose in the final scene—Hollywood censors would not have approved a movie in which a woman leaves her husband. But it is true that the scene was hastily written (and enacted in front of a miniature plane with midget crewmen). It was Bogart himself who came up with the line "Here's looking at you, kid," while he was teaching Bergman to play poker between scenes.

Three weeks after the movie wrapped, Bogart was called back to the studio to dub a final line of scripted dialogue, spoken to the French cop who

Rick will join in fighting the Nazis: "Louis, I think this is the beginning of a beautiful friendship." Another potential last-minute change could have occurred when music supervisor Max Steiner wanted to replace "As Time Goes By" with a new song. That would have required reshooting a scene with Bergman, though, and the actress had already cut her hair for her upcoming role in *For Whom the Bell Tolls*, so the change wasn't made.

The troubled film was released on Thanksgiving Day 1942—eighteen days after Allied troops came ashore at the real Casablanca. *Casablanca* was not an immediate smash, but thanks in part to the hit song, it steadily built an audience. It would eventually win three Academy Awards, including Best Picture, Best Director, and (yes) Best Adapted Screenplay. ★

Casablanca was released in 1942, when Hollywood production codes forbade depiction of a woman leaving her husband.
Universal Images Group/Getty Images

42

IT'S A WONDERFUL LIFE

Is Frank Capra's holiday favorite sentimental—or cynical?

*A*s a film critic, I'm often asked to name my favorite movie. I always answer *It's a Wonderful Life*—not because the 1946 flick is a heartwarming Christmas chestnut, but because it's a superbly crafted depiction of the dark contradictions in the American dream.

It's a Wonderful Life has practically become wrapping paper for our feelings about faith and family. There are commemorative Christmas ornaments, porcelain figurines, and even—in a scheme that would surely delight the money-grubbing character Mr. Potter—lottery tickets. Yet the film is not a Norman Rockwell–style sketch of small-town life. After the wake-up call of World War II, director Frank Capra jettisoned much of his trademark sentimentality and dove into cold, dark waters—just as Jimmy Stewart's character George Bailey does when he reaches the nadir of his despair.

It took a number of years for *Wonderful Life* to reach theaters. In 1939, Philip Van Doren Stern wrote a 4,000-word short story called *The Greatest Gift* about a small-town banker who wishes he had never been born. An angel grants his wish, and the man poses as a door-to-door salesman to see how his wife would have fared without him. In 1943, after Stern couldn't find a publisher for his story, he sent it as a Christmas card to 200 friends. Eventually it traveled to RKO Studios in Hollywood, which purchased the rights for $10,000.

It's a Wonderful Life received mixed reviews and only made $3.3 million (against a $3.7 million budget) during its initial box office run. RKO Pictures/ Getty Images

RKO sold the rights to Capra, the hit-making director of 1934's *It Happened One Night,* who was starting his own independent production company called Liberty Films. Several writers contributed to the script, including an uncredited Dorothy Parker and Capra himself. The director had just completed a stint as a wartime documentarian, and he poured some of his own experiences into the project. The movie was filmed in the sweltering summer of 1946 in Encino, California. The set was one of the largest ever built, with seventy-five buildings along a three-block Main Street.

The setting of the original story was never specified, but a good case could be made that the movie locale "Bedford Falls" was inspired by the town of Seneca Falls, New York. The film contains several references to nearby cities in New York State, including Elmira, Rochester, and Buffalo (the latter, famously, in the song "Buffalo Gals"). While Capra was contemplating the project, he is alleged to have stopped for a haircut in Seneca Falls, near the town where his mother lived. Seneca Falls, like Bedford Falls, has a bridge across a river, where a plaque describes how a good Samaritan dove into the icy waters to save a drowning woman. (The town now has an *It's a Wonderful Life* Christmas festival and museum.)

The story of a hard-pressed housing developer who is deprived of his dreams and punished for his good deeds featured the unprecedented sight of a male movie star, Jimmy Stewart, driven to tears by misfortune. (Cary Grant had been considered for the lead role, but then Grant committed to a similar supernatural Christmas movie called *The Bishop's Wife*.) Stewart had flown bombing missions during the war, and in his return to the big screen, many of the actor's tears were real.

Almost every moment of joy in George Bailey's life is disrupted by the hard slap of tragedy. A moonlight serenade with beautiful Mary Hatch (Donna Reed) ends with the death of George's father, forcing the son to take over the struggling Bailey Brothers Building and Loan Association and forgo a planned trip to Europe; George's chance to go to college is thwarted by the board of directors; and the holiday homecoming of George's war-hero brother is interrupted by the loss of a bank deposit. Mr. Potter (a delectably evil Lionel Barrymore), the rich ogre who finds and keeps the money, is never punished. Even George and Mary's first kiss, which is one of the most romantic scenes in movie history, is unnerving. After George refuses a ground-floor position at a plastics factory and tells Mary that he doesn't want to get married to anyone, ever, he succumbs to her tearful embrace—and a lifetime of duty.

The film received mixed reviews and did not break even at the box office. Although it was nominated for five Academy Awards, it was shut out, losing Best Picture to the coming-home tearjerker *The Best Years of Our Lives*. (*It's a Wonderful Life* did win a special award for its snowfall effects, which were achieved with a mix of fire-retardant, soap, and instant mashed potatoes.) Nevertheless, for years, Stewart and Capra described *It's a Wonderful Life* as their best work.

When the film's copyright expired in 1974, television stations determined that they were free to air it repeatedly. Thus, a movie that was not a big hit when it was first released became a Christmas-season perennial. It was not unusual for several stations to air the film in the same week— or even on the same day. (Since 1993, Hollywood lawyers have reasserted copyright claims to the original story and the background music, effectively limiting how often the film can be aired and whether it can be remade. So we're not likely to see a teen version called *My So-Called Wonderful Life*.)

In the years before home video and cable re-popularized old movies, the frequent TV screenings of *It's a Wonderful Life* made it a relatively accessible film for scholars to analyze. Some argued that the seemingly sentimental movie embodied psychological conflicts that would loom large in the postwar generation: between adventure and domesticity, between the individual and the community, between success and humility. The dramatic close-ups and the unleashed lawlessness of the "Pottersville" segment (when George sees what would have happened if he had never been born) hinted at the emerging genre of film noir. The theme of disillusionment with the American dream would be echoed a few years later in Arthur Miller's 1949 play *Death of a Salesman*.

The film's Christmas Eve ending, in which the community comes to George's aid with a bushel of money, is widely considered a happy one. But George's legal and financial troubles are not over, and he still faces an uncertain future.

Capra deleted a scene in which the greedy banker gets punished, a comeuppance for which many Americans are still waiting. ★

43

THE GRADUATE

Does a casting agent deserve the diploma?

*T*he success of 1967's *The Graduate* can be summed up in one word: casting. Yet even though Dustin Hoffman became an instant star as the college grad who is a little worried about his future, director Mike Nichols was more than a little worried about giving him the role.

The list of performers who were up for roles in *The Graduate* is both long and blurry. Seemingly every American actor in his twenties was considered for the role of protagonist Benjamin Braddock, and every actress in her forties was in the running for the part of his older lover, Mrs. Robinson. What Nichols ended up with were two performers in their thirties. And finding them wasn't easy.

Among the more intriguing contenders was Burt Ward, better known as Robin, the boy-wonder sidekick in the television series *Batman*. In his autobiography, Ward insisted that he was offered the part but could not get out of his TV contract. Easier to believe are the rumors that two of Hollywood's handsomest men were the leading contenders. Warren Beatty chose to concentrate on *Bonnie and Clyde*, which he was producing as well as starring in, but Robert Redford considered himself a natural choice. Nichols seemed to agree. In the 1963 Charles Webb novel, the Braddocks are Beverly Hills WASPs, and Ben is blonde and six feet tall. Nichols and screenwriter Buck Henry referred to the family as the Surfboards.

Dustin Hoffman was hardly the first choice to play Benjamin Braddock. Before casting began, producer Lawrence Turman created a wish list that included major stars like Steve McQueen, Warren Beatty, and Robert Redford.
Getty Images

Redford tested for the part of Benjamin alongside Candice Bergen, who was auditioning for the role of Ben's age-appropriate love interest Elaine Robinson. Redford thought the test had gone well, and he pressured Nichols, who had directed him on Broadway in *Barefoot in the Park*, to give him the part. Nichols ultimately decided that Redford couldn't convincingly play a loser, and he turned his attention to actors with comedic character faces.

Charles Grodin gave what Henry said was the best reading, but it didn't translate to film. Conversely, Hoffman, whom Nichols had seen in an off-Broadway play, gave a clumsy reading opposite Katharine Ross (who was also vying for the role of Elaine, as were Barbara Hershey and *True Grit*'s Kim Darby), but the playback on film was astonishing. Nichols later said that Hoffman was as visually arresting as Elizabeth Taylor, whom Nichols had recently directed in *Who's Afraid of Virginia Woolf?* (1966). He instantly decided that Benjamin should be the black sheep in a family that had hidden its Jewishness. (As a consolation prize, Nichols gave Grodin a role in 1970's *Catch-22*. A few years later, Grodin would break through in a mirror image of *The Graduate*, *The Heartbreak Kid*, directed by Nichols' comedy partner, Elaine May.)

The chronically insecure Hoffman, shocked by the job offer and convinced that Nichols was making a mistake, nonetheless accepted the role. (In doing so, he had to turn down an offer to play the Hitler-loving playwright in Mel Brooks' film *The Producers*.)

For Mr. and Mrs. Robinson, Nichols approached Doris Day and Ronald Reagan. Day wouldn't risk her wholesome reputation by playing a cradle-robbing adulteress, and Reagan had his sights set on politics. Resisting a plea from aging sex symbol Ava Gardner, Nichols offered the role of Mrs. Robinson to Anne Bancroft—Mrs. Mel Brooks—whom the director had once dated. She was thirty-six—only six years older than Hoffman. Thirty-seven-year-old Gene Hackman, who was hired to play her husband, was fired after a few days of shooting because Nichols thought he didn't seem old enough. (Hackman was replaced by Murray Hamilton.) Hoffman was a close friend (and ex-roommate) of Hackman, and the firing struck the star of the movie as a bad omen.

Hoffman was paid only $17,000 for his work—compared to $200,000 for Bancroft—and in the same month that the movie was released, he was spotted at the New York unemployment office collecting a $55 check. Within just a few months, the star of *The Graduate* had earned the first of seven Oscar nominations. Unlike the character that made his career, he would never have to worry about his future again. ★

44

THE GODFATHER

How many offers did Francis Ford Coppola refuse?

$\mathcal{M}$any film aficionados consider *The Godfather* to be a perfect movie. On the Internet Movie Database, the most popular movie website in the world, visitors have voted it as the second-best film of all time, just ahead of *The Godfather Part II*. (Surprisingly, the top spot in the poll is reserved for the prison-break crowd-pleaser *The Shawshank Redemption*.) The American Film Institute also ranks *The Godfather* as the second best film, behind *Citizen Kane*. The magazines *Entertainment Weekly* and *Empire* both rank *The Godfather* No. 1.

It's hard to imagine Francis Ford Coppola's Mob epic with a different director or cast. But if the studio suits had prevailed, Coppola's version of *The Godfather* would be sleeping with the fishes.

Desperate for a hit, Paramount optioned Mario Puzo's novel before it even published. When the book did come out in 1969, it was a worldwide smash, selling 10 million copies. *Variety* called the pre-publication movie rights option "the prime deal for a bestseller in modern film history," as Paramount only paid $80,000 (compared to $400,000 paid for Philip Roth's *Portnoy's Complaint*, the film adaptation of which was a "true fiasco" according to Roger Ebert).

Executives at the studio initially thought that the young Italian-American Coppola would be a good choice to adapt it because of his ethnic

heritage—and his indebtedness. Coppola had won an Oscar for writing *Patton* (1970), but the film-school graduate was an easily controlled apprentice director who needed money after producing his friend George Lucas' sci-fi flop *THX 1138*.

However, after the novel remained atop the bestseller list for more than a year, the studio decided that the movie needed a big-name director. Attempts to hire one failed. *Patton* director Franklin Shaffner, *Bonnie and Clyde* director Arthur Penn, and Italian action auteur Sergio Leone all thought the novel glorified criminals and declined to participate. In the spring of 1971, Coppola was offered the job.

While the studio wanted a shoot-'em-up set in the 1970s, Coppola envisioned the organized-crime saga as a period piece and a critique of capitalist greed, with high production values and a prestige cast. The director's top two choices for the title role of Don Vito Corleone were British stage legend Laurence Olivier and mercurial method actor Marlon Brando. Olivier declined, citing ill health, and the studio balked at Brando, who was only forty-seven and whose recent films had flopped. Paramount favored Ernest Borgnine, the Oscar winner for *Marty* who had starred in the television series *McHale's Navy*. Edward G. Robinson, Anthony Quinn, George C. Scott, and even nightclub comedian Danny Thomas were also considered.

From left, Robert Duvall, John Cazale, Gianni Russo, Talia Shire, Morgana King, Marlon Brando, and James Caan in *The Godfather*. Russo allegedly used organized crime connections to win the role of Carlo Rizzi. © *Moviestore Collection Ltd/Alamy*

Frank Sinatra, who hated the book because the character of Mob-connected singer Johnny Fontane was rumored to be based on him, nonetheless lobbied the director for the lead role, in vain. Coppola's handwritten list of backup candidates included John Marley (who would ultimately play the movie producer who gets a very real horse head placed in his bed) and Frank DeKova, a veteran character actor who played Chief Wild Eagle on the Western sitcom *F-Troop*.

Brando and Borgnine were the two finalists. Brando was forced to audition, and after he gave an impressive reading with cotton wads stuffed in his cheeks, he was offered the part, albeit at union scale. (For the actual filming, he was given a dental implant and a pay raise to $50,000.)

The studio wanted a heartthrob such as Ryan O'Neal, Robert Redford, or James Caan for the key role of war-hero-turned-mobster Michael Corleone. Coppola insisted on the lesser-known Italian-American actor Al Pacino, who had just signed to do a Mob comedy called *The Gang That Couldn't Shoot Straight*. The studio agreed to hire Pacino as long as Caan was cast as hot-headed Sonny Corleone. Coppola was ultimately satisfied with the cast (which included his sister, Talia Shire, as Connie Corleone) and crew (including his father, Carmine Coppola, in the music department).

Another lesser-known Italian-American actor, Robert De Niro, had signed on to play the ill-fated driver Paulie, but with Coppola's blessing he bowed out of the project to take Pacino's role in *The Gang That Couldn't Shoot Straight*. That freed De Niro to return to the franchise as young Vito Corleone in *The Godfather: Part II*, for which he won the Academy Award for Best Supporting Actor despite speaking barely a word of English in the role.

When word of the production started to spread, Coppola was beset by meddlers. Crime boss Joe Colombo insisted that Coppola remove all reference to "the Mafia" from the script the director had co-written with Puzo and hire certain goons as extras. More galling, Paramount executive Robert Evans wanted Coppola to add more violence, and Evans kept veteran director Elia Kazan on retainer in case the studio was dissatisfied with Coppola's work.

Although Coppola's high-wire work methods would take their toll on the set of *Apocalypse Now* (1979), he finished *The Godfather* on time and under his hard-won budget of $6 million. The film was released in March 1972 and went on to earn $130 million in the United States and an equal amount overseas. It was nominated for eleven Academy Awards and won three: Best Picture, Best Adapted Screenplay, and Best Actor. (Brando sent a surrogate, Sacheen Littlefeather, to refuse the award, in protest of Hollywood's treatment of Native Americans.)

Among the volumes of trivia generated by *The Godfather*, perhaps the most ironic is this: despite being the ultimate New York movie, it was the first Best Picture honoree to feature a scene set in Los Angeles (when the consigliere played by Robert Duvall makes the movie producer an offer he shouldn't refuse). It was also the first Best Picture winner to depict the film industry itself.

So was Coppola equating Hollywood with the Mafia? As they say in the neighborhood, if the cement shoes fit... ★

JAWS

Was young Steven Spielberg ingenious—or an intruder?

*I*n 1975, the thriller *Jaws* took a bite out of one summertime tradition—going to the beach—and spawned another: going to see blockbuster movies as soon as they open. But don't take the bait that director Steven Spielberg was a boy who bluffed his way onto the studio lot. He earned his seat in the captain's chair, and when his shark-attack movie was about to capsize, he proved himself a nimble navigator.

Spielberg was born in Cincinnati in 1946 and raised in suburbs in New Jersey and Arizona. As a kid he made Super-8 adventure movies, for which he charged neighbors twenty-five cents admission. His filmmaking grew more ambitious while he was working on a Boy Scout merit badge, prompting him, at age sixteen, to make a two-hour sci-fi flick called *Firelight* that screened at a Phoenix theater (and later inspired *Close Encounters of the Third Kind*).

That same year, Spielberg started working at Universal Studios in Los Angeles. Despite the stories he would tell in subsequent years, he didn't get the job after jumping from a tour tram or donning a business suit and barging past a security guard. Spielberg's father, an engineer at General Electric, had contacted a friend of a friend at the studio, who gave the pesky teenager a tour and later got him an unpaid clerical internship.

Spielberg made the most of the opportunity, and in subsequent summers he proved himself so useful that he was eventually offered the chance to direct episodes of the television shows *Night Gallery*, *Marcus Welby, M.D.*, and *Columbo*. That led to his feature-length breakthrough, a TV movie called *Duel* about a driver who is harassed by an 18-wheeler. It was released in theaters overseas, where it was a critical and box-office hit. Spielberg's theatrical debut in the United States was a movie called *The Sugarland Express*, in which Goldie Hawn flees a police dragnet to regain custody of her child.

In 1974, the twenty-eight-year-old director was offered the manuscript of a Peter Benchley novel called *Jaws* and the opportunity to turn it into a film. Spielberg imagined a kind of Godzilla movie and commissioned an effects team to build three mechanical great white sharks—one for left-side shots, one for right-side shots, and a complete twenty-five-foot-long model that he dubbed Bruce.

But when the sharks were transported to the shooting locale on Martha's Vineyard, Massachusetts, Spielberg discovered that salt water ate through the rubber skin and corroded the hydraulics. So he had to improvise. Although a few scenes utilized the mechanical sharks before they were jettisoned, most of the jolts in *Jaws* are caused by fear of a predator we rarely see. Spielberg positioned the camera at water level and signaled the shark's presence with a single fin, bobbing yellow barrels, or John Williams' ominous two-note crescendo. (He also cheated a little by having a normal-sized shark attack an underwater cage that contained a diminutive body double dressed to resemble Richard Dreyfuss.)

Jaws was given an immense publicity buildup and released on June 20, 1975, in more than 400 theaters. The wide release was an unprecedented strategy in an era when films would roll out slowly in showplace cinemas and gradually move to the suburbs. *Jaws* was an immediate hit, becoming the first film to earn $100 million in domestic box-office revenues. It earned an equal amount overseas.

Similar frenzies of buildup and seemingly endless ticket lines would recur for subsequent summer blockbusters including George Lucas' *Star Wars* (1977) and the Lucas-Spielberg collaboration *Raiders of the Lost Ark* (1981). Today, with the glut of multiplex theaters, it is not unusual for blockbusters to open on 4,000 screens on the same day, but *Jaws* remains the big fish of summer sensations. ★

Richard Dreyfuss, Robert Shaw, and "Bruce" (believed to have been named after Steven Spielberg's lawyer). *Universal Pictures/ Getty Images*

46

STAR WARS

Was George Lucas crazy like a fox?

George Lucas didn't become a billionaire by directing *Star Wars*. He did it by selling toys.

The *Star Wars* origin story is the stuff of legends. In 1971, USC film-school graduate Lucas expanded his senior project, *THX 1138*, into a sci-fi feature film about a mind-controlled drone. Although the movie was not a commercial success, it earned Lucas a development deal with United Artists. He presented the studio with two ideas: an autobiographical teenage-years remembrance called *American Graffiti* and an homage to the Flash Gordon serials called *The Star Wars*. UA rejected both ideas, but Universal Studios picked up *American Graffiti* and the twenty-six-year-old Lucas spent the next two years refining and shooting that script.

After *American Graffiti* was in the can, Lucas approached Alan Ladd Jr. at 20th Century Fox about *The Star Wars*. Although sci-fi was considered a risky genre, Ladd offered Lucas $150,000 to finish the script and direct it.

American Graffiti was released in August 1973, earning good reviews and considerable money. It gave Lucas the leverage to renegotiate his contract for *The Star Wars*. In lieu of a $500,000 director's fee, he wanted $175,000 up front, final cut of the film, 40 percent of the net box office, rights to any sequels, and rights to license and sell *The Star Wars* merchandise.

In those days, movie merchandise was not a big source of revenue, and 20th Century Fox still had a warehouse full of unsold toys from the 1967

Harrison Ford (Han Solo), Carrie Fisher (Princess Leia), Anthony Daniels (C-3PO), and Peter Mayhew (Chewbacca) on the set of *Star Wars Episode V: The Empire Strikes Back*, 1980. *© Sunset Boulevard/Corbis*

musical *Dr. Doolittle*. The studio executives agreed to Lucas' terms, probably thinking they had made a shrewd deal.

Lucas spent two years revising his script, based on Joseph Campbell's treatise *The Power of Myth*, Akira Kurosawa's 1958 film *The Hidden Fortress*, and countless comic books. During Lucas' rewriting process, a general named Luke Starkiller became a boy named Luke Skywalker. A smuggler, Han Solo, changed from a monster with gills and green skin to something resembling Harrison Ford.

Ford himself, who'd had a small role in *American Graffiti*, helped Lucas with the casting process. Lucas preferred to cast unknowns, so Mark Hamill beat out William Katt *(The Greatest American Hero)* for the role of Luke and Carrie Fisher was offered the role of Princess Leia instead of Sissy Spacek. When Lucas heard how Ford finessed the corny dialogue, he cast him as Han Solo over contenders such as Christopher Walken and Nick Nolte.

Throughout the trouble-plagued production in London and Tunisia, Ford continued to grumble about the dialogue. The oft-repeated legend is that he told the writer/director, "You can type this [stuff], George, but you sure can't say it."

Star Wars (the *"The"* was dropped during production) went over budget and fell behind schedule. Fox considered selling it to another distributor or pulling the plug altogether unless Lucas cooperated. Eventually Lucas delivered a movie that even his friend Brian De Palma and business mentor Francis Ford Coppola thought was a mediocre kiddie flick. When theater owners refused to book it, Fox threatened to withhold a potential blockbuster (and ultimate flop) called *The Other Side of Midnight* unless they also took *Star Wars*.

Lucas' movie opened on May 25, 1977, in about forty theaters. By the end of its first run, it had earned more than $300 million in North America (and when re-releases are factored in, it surpassed *Gone with the Wind* to become the highest-grossing film of all time). It was nominated for ten Oscars and won six.

Kenner Products, a toy company licensed to sell *Star Wars* action figures and other merchandise, was unprepared for the demand. At Christmastime, it sold empty boxes that could be redeemed for *Star Wars* items in the spring.

With his 40 percent stake in the net box office (which is an accounting trick that precludes print and advertising fees), Lucas earned about $40 million from the first *Star Wars* movie. Between 1977 and 1980 (when his contract allowed him to produce the sequel *The Empire Strikes Back* with his own money), he earned about $500 million from merchandise. It is estimated that the six movies in the series (all of which have been retitled to start with the brand name *Star Wars*) have generated more than $13 billion

in merchandising revenue. Lucas' unusually favorable box office stake; his revenues from the Indiana Jones franchise that he co-created with his friend Steven Spilberg; and his profits from the effects company Industrial Light & Magic, the sound company THX, and the video game company LucasArts have all contributed to Lucas' vast fortune. He annually ranks over Spielberg and Oprah Winfrey as the richest person in show business.

He is also the poster boy for intellectual property rights. If a toy company wants to sell a limited-edition light saber, or if Pepsi wants to use Darth Vader in a commercial, it has to make a personal appeal to Lucas, who gets either a lucrative fee or a percentage of sales. (In 2011, Lucas lost a court case in England that allowed the original designer of the movie's white storm trooper outfits to sell replicas there. The copyright restrictions still apply in the United States.)

Lucas, who is just as prone to rewriting his history as he is to re-editing his films, now says he wasn't psychic about the potential of *Star Wars* merchandise. He just wanted to make some cool T-shirts. ★

Even in a non-movie year, *Star Wars* is a cash cow. According to *The Hollywood Reporter*, 2010 *Star Wars* toy revenue exceeded $510 million. *Photograph by Gabriel Bouys. AFP/Getty Images*

47

TITANIC

Did James Cameron flee the country to make his mega-millions?

here do you suppose *Titanic* was filmed? In the frigid North Atlantic? On a Hollywood sound stage?

Try Mexico, a few miles south of Tijuana.

A century ago, economic factors (and year-round sunshine) sprouted a film industry in greater Los Angeles. Those same factors have since imperiled it. As the cost of making movies increased, partly due to union wages, the cost of basic filmmaking technology decreased, and technicians outside of Hollywood learned how to use it. As early as the 1960s, some studio films were farmed out to overseas facilities such as Cinecittà Studios in Rome.

By the 1980s, cost-conscious producers were looking northward to Canada, where talented crews spoke English, the costs of food and lodging were relatively cheap, and the government offered tax breaks for visiting filmmakers. (If you've ever been to Toronto, a diverse metropolis that hosts what is arguably the most important film festival in the world, you may have seen streetscapes that have doubled for New York City in countless movies.) Other locales in North America and Europe followed suit, dangling incentives in front of film producers who used to call Hollywood home.

In the mid-1990s, Canadian producer and director James Cameron was determined to make a film about the sinking of the ocean liner the RMS *Titanic*. The story had been told before, in the fine 1958 British film

Titanic topped the charts for fifteen straight weeks and turned Leonardo DiCaprio into an international superstar. *20th Century-Fox/Photofest*

A Night to Remember. Interest in the sinking was rekindled in 1985 when oceanographers discovered the site in the North Atlantic where 1,500 people perished.

Cameron, the director of the sci-fi flicks *Aliens* and *The Terminator*, got his feet wet in aquatic cinema with *The Abyss*. He knew that making *Titanic* would be expensive.

Cameron scouted seaside locations around the world where he could build his sets and make his movie without paying American wages and taxes. He settled upon a forty-acre site in Rosarito, Mexico, eighteen miles south of the U.S. border. In one hundred days, 20th Century Fox built a complex there with the largest outdoor water tank in the world (17 million gallons), the largest indoor tank (5 million gallons), numerous soundstages, construction sheds, and storage for more than a thousand wardrobes.

The centerpiece of the production was a massive model of the starboard side of the Titanic. At 90 percent of the original ship's size, the model was 775 feet long and ten stories high.

Filming in Mexico reduced the budget to "only" $200 million. Most of the key personnel were Americans and many of them commuted across the border (in the days before a passport was mandatory). And Cameron was able to restrict snoopers' access to the facility, thus miminizing the bad publicity about the crew's long hours and on-set injuries.

His gamble paid off. *Titanic*, released in December 1997, became the highest-grossing film of all time (not adjusted for inflation) and won a record-tying eleven Academy Awards.

For a few years, Fox maintained the Rosarito facility as a combination tourist attraction and production hub. Much of *Master and Commander*, the first *X-Men* movie, and Tim Burton's remake of *Planet of the Apes* were filmed there. But eventually Fox sold the property to Mexican entrepreneurs, who run it today as a rental facility called Baja Film Studios.

Tourists are still invited to visit and see how movies are made, but because of the new passport regulations, there are fewer day-trippers from the United States. On the afternoon when my wife and I visited, we were the only tourists there, and the young tour guides were surprised to see us. We got hands-on demonstrations of green-screen backgrounds, makeup techniques, and the optical effects that can make a bathtub boat look like an ocean liner. Then we toured the restaurant where Rose (Kate Winslet) dined with her snooty relatives and the cell where Jack (Leonardo DiCaprio) was chained to the bars as the ship sank. We even posed on the stand-alone bow where Jack and Rose gazed out to sea. We felt like the king and queen of the world. ★

PART 5
The Movie
INDUSTRY

HOLLYWOOD, CALIFORNIA, USA

Where exactly is the movie mecca?

*A*lthough the name is synonymous with the American film industry, the physical place called Hollywood is merely a neighborhood within Los Angeles, the way Greenwich Village is a neighborhood in New York City. And within the place called Hollywood there is only one major movie studio: Paramount Pictures.

It wasn't always that way. In 1887, an area of fig and avocado groves northwest of downtown Los Angeles was named Hollywood by Daeida Wilcox, the wife of Kansas developer and ardent prohibitionist Harvey Wilcox. (She had heard the name from a woman she met on a train, who called her summer home Hollywood.) Mr. and Mrs. Wilcox sold land to vacationers and offered it for free to anyone who agreed to build a church. The town of Hollywood was an autonomous legal entity from 1903 to 1910, during which liquor and movie theaters were banned there. Hollywood was then absorbed into Los Angeles, a city of 100,000 that was on the verge of an unprecedented boom.

In the 1910s, moviemakers flocked to Hollywood (and to a lesser extent, Jacksonville, Florida) for the sunny weather and to evade the patent attorneys working for Thomas Edison, who insisted that he had invented the core technology of motion pictures and was entitled to royalties on all films. By 1915, greater Los Angeles had replaced New York as the filmmaking capital of the world. Major studios within the Hollywood neighborhood included Paramount and RKO Pictures, on Melrose Avenue; Warner Bros. on Santa Monica Boulevard; and Columbia Pictures, on the site of the pioneering Centaur Studio at Sunset and Gower. (The biggest of the studios, MGM, was in suburban Culver City, about eight miles away. Fox was nearby in West Los Angeles.) Hollywood was like a factory town, with Craftsman-style bungalows for the set painters, costumers, and character actors who kept the wheels turning.

After World War II, the self-contained studio system broke down. More films were made by independent producers, and often, for the sake of realism, they were filmed at out-of-town locations rather than studio back lots and soundstages. While the Hollywood neighborhood retained some editing, equipment-rental, and television facilities, most of the movie studios were gone.

RKO, which had made *King Kong* (1933) and *Citizen Kane* (1941), was bought first by Howard Hughes and then by the General Tire and Rubber Company before it went out of the movie business in 1959. After the costly debacle of *Cleopatra* in 1963, Fox sold most of its studio real estate to the developers of a suburb called Century City. Columbia moved with Warner Bros. to the San Fernando Valley town of Burbank, near horror-flick specialist Universal Studios.

Today, the lack of actual movie production is one reason why many tourists are disappointed when they visit the place called Hollywood. Yes, there are wax museums, celebrity footprints in the courtyard outside Grauman's Chinese Theatre, costumed lookalikes who will charge you to pose with them, and terracotta stars on the sidewalk (about 2,500 of them, for which the honorees pay $25,000), but there are very few actual stars on the streets or in the restaurants. Despite some recent redevelopment, including numerous trendy nightclubs and the mall at Hollywood and Highland that is now the site of the annual Oscars ceremony, the multi-ethnic neighborhood is mostly working class. The leery stars look down from the inaccessible hilltops or hide in gated enclaves in Malibu.

Intrepid tourists still buy inaccurate maps that promise to guide them to the stars' homes and take double-decker bus tours through the gauntlet of T-shirt shops on Hollywood Boulevard, but what they really need is a time machine. The fabled corner of Hollywood and Vine was once the location of the Brown Derby restaurant where, in the *I Love Lucy* episode "L.A. at Last," Lucy Ricardo causes a plate of food to be dumped on heartthrob William Holden. Today, visitors find only an unremarkable parking lot. ★

Hollywood is just one neighborhood in the Los Angeles metropolis. *Andy Z./Shutterstock.com*

FOREIGN MARKETS

Does Hollywood speak the international language?

*T*he United States certainly isn't the only country that makes movies, cars, or computers, although for decades it dominated those markets. Today entertainment is one of the few industries in which the U.S. is still the world leader. The percentage of entertainment revenue that is generated by Americans sitting in movie theaters, however, is undeniably shrinking.

More optimistically, you could say that the pie is expanding.

In 2010, Hollywood collected 67 percent of its box-office revenues outside of the United States. A quarter century ago, that number was just 25 percent. The shift is one reason why studios now invest so heavily in summertime sequels and special-effects spectaculars—those movies don't rely heavily on dialogue and are easy to export. In the era of globalization, it's not unusual for an American blockbuster to have its red-carpet premiere overseas and to play for several weeks before it opens in Ohio or Oklahoma.

Since the end of World War II, American movies have flourished in industrialized countries such as France, Germany, Japan, and the United Kingdom, even though those nations have healthy homegrown film industries. In the new millennium, movie-theater construction is booming in developing countries with growing middle classes, including Brazil, Russia, India, and China. While China, the biggest market on earth, has about 6,000 movie screens (compared to 39,000 in the United States), the Asian powerhouse is adding four new screens per day.

But as with everything else, there is heightened competition. China, where *Avatar* smashed records, permits only twenty foreign films per year in its theaters, which mostly rely on movies from Hong Kong. France has cultural quotas as well. And the affluent Japanese seem to be losing their taste for imports, which now account for less than half of the country's movie revenue, down from 73 percent a decade ago.

Most notably, the huge market in movie-crazed India is dominated by domestic fare, which generates 90 percent of that nation's box office. India actually produces far more feature films than America—about 1,300 theatrical releases per year, compared with about 300 in the United States. (A small but growing number of "Bollywood" movies are produced by Hollywood studios, which lend their production expertise to Hindi-language films that most Americans will never hear about.) Other countries with surprisingly vigorous film industries include Nigeria and Egypt.

Hollywood theatrical releases not only compete with other countries' films; they also compete with other forms of movie-viewing. In the United States, the sale, rental, and streaming of movies for home consumption account for more revenue than theatrical screenings: $18 billion versus $10 billion. Blockbuster video stores may be fading out, but those dollar-a-night Redbox kiosks at grocery stores, gas stations, and fast-food restaurants are big business. And entities such as Netflix and Hulu have negotiated deals to stream recent hits within weeks of their theatrical release. (Overseas, a lot of potential box-office revenue is lost to pirates who bootleg DVDs of Hollywood blockbusters before those movies even open in the States.)

Another threat to theaters is video games, the market for which is now roughly equal to the market for DVDs. Their tremendous popularity is one reason why so many games are adapted into films (and vice versa). Nipping at the heels of home video and gaming is the porn industry, which generates about $14 billion a year.

Of course, nobody feels sorry for studios, which are owned by multinational conglomerates with interests in publishing, cable TV, and consumer electronics. But if you want to vote for certain kinds of entertainment in certain kinds of settings, providers speak the international language of cash. ★

Mumbai is the center of "Bollywood," the Hindi-language film industry. Bollywood is the largest film industry in India, which is in turn the largest producer of films in the world. © *Catherine Karnow/Corbis*

50

DRIVE-IN MOVIES

Has the sun set on the era of outdoor movies?

*T*here are 400 drive-in movie theaters in small towns and big cities across America. That's more than most people realize but quite a bit less than there used to be. At the peak of the drive-in phenomenon, in the late 1950s, there were 4,000 outdoor theaters in the United States, accounting for one third of the nation's movie screens.

Drive-ins have been around since 1933, when an inventor in Camden, New Jersey, named Richard Hollingshead patented the idea. His patent did not cover the concept of showing movies in a parking lot; rather, it proposed parking cars on little mounds that would raise the sightline above the cars in front of them. Hollingshead advertised the drive-in as a way for families to attend movies without having to hire babysitters.

The idea was not an immediate success. The first generation of drive-ins used large, screen-mounted speakers—which drew the wrath of neighbors—and the studios, which owned the majority of indoor theaters, denied drive-ins the right to show first-run movies.

But after World War II, the combination of suburban development, a growing population, a thriving auto industry, and the invention of the window-hung, individual speaker ignited a boom in drive-in construction. Even when the outdoor theaters were stuck with cheaply made or second-run movies, American families flocked to the so-called "ozoners," where they could enjoy live music, miniature golf, and even laundry facilities before darkness fell and the movies began. The concession stands offered amenities that were not generally available at indoor theaters, including bottle warmers, chicken platters, and a new delicacy called pizza that many Americans had never tasted before.

From 1950 to 1954, new drive-ins opened at a rate of one per day. Even as indoor theaters saw their attendance eroded by television, drive-ins kept the film industry profitable. They were among the first businesses in America to cater to teenagers (a demographic term that did not even exist until the era of the drive-in). Drive-ins specialized in youth-culture movies, horror films, and other exploitation fare that they could obtain cheaply through independent distributors. With so many teens canoodling in convertibles, moralists denounced the venues as "passion pits."

After the courts forced the movie studios to divest themselves of their theater holdings and to open their distribution to impartial bids, some drive-ins were

"It's such a groovy place to talk and maybe watch a show."

— "Drive-in," by The Beach Boys

able to obtain better movies. Yet it really didn't matter what they showed. Car-crazy Americans wanted the special ambience of the drive-in, and the movie was only part of the show. And not just Americans—there were drive-ins in Canada, South Africa, Australia, and elsewhere around the world.

But then in 1966, the U.S. government passed the Uniform Time Act, which standardized daylight savings time. This effectively added an extra hour of sunshine before the movies could begin and thus narrowed the time window for attracting families to double features. Drive-ins also had to compete with a pair of new inventions that offered easy access to recent feature films: cable television and videocassettes.

In the 1970s and 1980s, drive-ins disappeared by the thousands. In suburban areas, particularly in the Sun Belt, the land was more valuable for housing. In the Midwest, many small-town drive-ins were razed to make room for Wal-Mart stores. Those owners who tried to stay in business were forced to pay taxes on the inflated value of the land and to buy extra insurance to cover their playground facilities. To stay alive, many of the remaining drive-ins tinkered with the formula. The short-lived Autoscope Drive-In near Joplin, Missouri, offered individual TV-sized screens for each car. Some theaters switched to X-rated fare. But the inexorable decline continued.

Although the commercial heyday of the drive-ins is over, remaining theaters are now riding the same wave of nostalgia that has buoyed the towns along Route 66. When the U.S. Postal Service sponsored a vote for a new stamp to represent the 1950s, the drive-in theater was the overwhelming first choice for its subject, ahead of such icons as *I Love Lucy* and rock 'n' roll music.

And surprisingly, the drive-ins that have remained in business are thriving, as families discover they still have an alternative to television. The shrewdest drive-ins offer a comprehensive entertainment experience. Many sponsor classic-car shows and dusk-to-dawn horror marathons. Some double as swap meets (including one in Fort Lauderdale, Florida, with fourteen screens—and circus acts). Drive-ins in Monte Vista, Colorado, and Fairlee, Vermont, have hotels on the back row of the property where guests can watch the movie through their windows while the sound is piped directly into the rooms. In recent years, new drive-ins have been built from Buffalo to Beijing, and dozens of old drive-ins have risen from the dead. Almost all drive-ins now transmit sound directly to FM car radios, rivaling the audio of an indoor theater, and many have screens that are bigger than those of IMAX theaters. (And in recent years, outdoor movie screenings in public places have become a genuine phenomenon, as cities attract filmgoers and their folding chairs to cinema under the stars.)

As studios phase out film reels in favor of cheaper-to-ship hard drives that must be played on expensive digital projectors, the 400 remaining drive-ins face a new technical and financial challenge. But to paraphrase B-movie bard Joe Bob Briggs, as long as there are summer nights, the drive-in will never die. ★

A Utah drive-in showing *The Ten Commandments*, 1958. *J. R. Eyerman/ Getty Images*

51

THE POPCORN BUSINESS

Do theaters get fat on ticket sales?

$\mathcal{I}$f you own a theater, you're not in the movie business. You're in the popcorn business.

It's not unusual for movie fans to complain about ticket prices that can top ten dollars for an adult admission and seem to be perpetually on the rise. Patrons may assume that if they complain to the manager, they're being heard by the people who are profiting. But most of the price of a movie ticket is heading out of town, to the studio that produced the film and (sometimes) the superstar who agreed to act in it.

In the 1980s, suburbs and multiplexes proliferated in America, and metro areas that used to debut a movie in a single showplace cinema could offer a new Spielberg or Lucas blockbuster in numerous venues on the same day. Studios, which owned their own theaters until a court-ordered crackdown in 1948, realized during the 1980s that they could cash in on high demand, and they renegotiated their deals with locally owned chains. If exhibitors wanted to screen a guaranteed hit, they would have to agree to give most of the money to Hollywood.

The split became lopsided in the 1990s and 2000s, when the number of screens—and the number of movies—mushroomed. Studios insisted on a stair-step approach, in which they would earn 70 percent of the revenues in the first week, 60 percent in the second, 50 percent in the third, and so

on. The secret advantage was that hot movies, opening on so many screens that no one had to wait more than a few minutes to see them, would cool off after a few weeks, by which time there was inevitably another blockbuster that merited a 70/30 split.

In the new millennium, theater owners have borne another expense. Most Hollywood movies are now shot on digital video, and it is cheaper for the studios to send the finished products to theaters as small hard drives or digital downloads instead of reels of celluloid film, which are relatively expensive to duplicate and ship. But to show digital movies, particularly in 3-D, theaters have to invest in special projectors. Digital 3-D projectors can cost $100,000.

Concession stand, 1949.
Peter Stackpole/
Getty Images

In recent years, many theater owners have renegotiated the deals, getting studios to subsidize the cost of digital projectors and to recalibrate the split of the ticket price. Today it's not unusual for a studio to agree to a flat percentage for the (short) life of a movie in a theater. Depending on the movie and the clout of the exhibitor, the studio might take 55 to 60 percent of the revenue.

When a star is foolish enough to sign a contract for a percentage of the net profits, he or she eventually learns that the term is deliberately hard to define. The studios hire expensive accountants who can prove that hit movies that incur advertising and promotion expenses don't earn a nickel of net profit. (Paramount tried to prove this with the 1988 Eddie Murphy blockbuster *Coming to America.* When political satirist Art Buchwald filed a lawsuit against the film's producers, contending that the idea for the film had been his own, the studio claimed—in vain—that the movie hadn't recouped its costs.) Savvy stars like Jack Nicholson and Tom Cruise insist on gross-profit participation (i.e., a cut of every box-office dollar, before the studio expenses). In such cases, an actor can earn tens or even hundreds of millions of dollars.

That doesn't leave much for your friendly neighborhood nickelodeon. Theaters in fact make most of their money from concessions.

In the early days of silent movies, food was sold outside of the theater by independent vendors. It wasn't until the Great Depression that exhibitors realized they could make a few cents on sweets like bonbons and Baby Ruth candy bars. During World War II, sugar was rationed, so theater owners figured out how to peddle popcorn without setting their movie palaces on fire.

After the war, television took a big bite out of movie attendance, yet concession sales skyrocketed. Exhibitors showed trailers that touted their treats, particularly at places such as drive-ins that offered double features with intermissions. "Let's all go to the lobby" was an overt advertising slogan to encourage snacking, but more subliminal messages were spread as well—phrases like "Eat Popcorn" and "Drink Coca-Cola" were spliced into the films. (The practice was banned by the FCC in 1974.) In recent years, theaters have actively promoted large-sized sodas, popcorn, and candy, which have high profit margins.

Even with gimmicks like 3-D (a ticket surcharge from which the studios take the lion's share), theaters still live or die on food sales. So if there are polite ushers, bright projectors, and clean restrooms at your favorite local cinema, consider expressing your thanks by buying some Jujubes. ★

52

THE AUDIENCE

Do grown-ups go to the movies?

Two-thirds of Americans go to the movies at least once a year. That number includes a lot of adults. It just takes them longer to get there.

If you go to the multiplex on the opening night of a summer movie, you'll see a lot of teenagers and twenty-somethings. According to the Motion Picture Association of America, while people ages twelve to twenty-four represent about 18 percent of the American population, they are responsible for about 33 percent of the billion-plus movie tickets that are sold each year. Those young moviegoers can ensure that a heavily advertised blockbuster has a big opening weekend. They're also social networkers who can quickly warn their peers about a potential stinker.

Moviegoers over thirty-five, who average about four tickets per year (versus seven tickets for the twelve- to twenty-four-year-olds), are more likely to read reviews or wait for a face-to-face report from a friend they trust. Fortunately for those who are pestered by talking teenagers, many of the films that appeal to adults are saved for a special time of year: the winter, when kids are in school and most of the year-end award contenders open in theaters.

Many of those prestige pictures debut in September at the Toronto International Film Festival—which rivals Cannes as the most important movie showcase of the year—and build buzz through the autumn. By December, the Oscar hopefuls have opened in the major markets, and by January they are playing in the provinces, where they settle into long engagements. Movies with "legs" that allow grown-ups to catch up with them can produce more income for theaters than meteoric blockbusters.

Fans at the U.K. premiere of *Harry Potter and the Deathly Hallows Part 2.* More than half of the U.S. audience for the film was over age twenty-five, having grown up with the Harry Potter franchise.
© *Paul Cunningham/Corbis*

Although it sometimes seems that teenage boys have bullied Hollywood into releasing an endless string of superhero, slasher, and stoner flicks, the marketers keep an eye on the ladies, too. It was adult women who made *Gone with the Wind, The Sound of Music,* and *Titanic* the highest-grossing films of their eras and made the low-budget comedy *My Big Fat Greek Wedding* one of the most profitable. In 2011, women flocked to *Bridesmaids,* which was (imprecisely) billed as the first sex comedy for women, and the housemaid soap-opera *The Help,* which debuted behind the superhero movie *Captain America: The First Avenger* but continued to clean up for months. (Meanwhile, adult men watch TV sports while holding out for the latest Eastwood, Stallone, or Willis movies.)

Keep in mind that it's women for whom the Oscars, with their red-carpet fashion show and commercials predominantly aimed at mothers, are designed. Women comprised 50 percent of the American movie audience in 2010, and in some recent years that number has been as high as 55 percent. The horror-movie market would shrivel and die if boys couldn't talk their girlfriends into going.

Of course, the bottom line is money. African-American producer/director/actor Tyler Perry has built an empire—and an actual production facility in Atlanta—on the opening-week grosses for his urban-centric movies, which rarely screen for critics but attract a devoted, opening-night audience of people over thirty.

In 2011, MPAA statistics showed that the fastest-growing group of moviegoers was Hispanic men and women, both young and old. Hispanics comprise 16 percent of the American population and 29 percent of "frequent" moviegoers (those who go once or more per month). If current trends continue, don't be surprised if we see a spoof called *My Big Fat Latino Bridesmaids*—in 3-D. ★

53

THE CRITICS

Do reviewers deserve a thumbs-up—or blame for dumbing us down?

When it comes to movies, everyone's a critic, but only a few people get paid for their opinions. As of this writing, there are about 120 full-time film critics at American newspapers and magazines. I'm lucky to be one of them. As I always say when readers send me hate mail, in matters of personal taste, there is no right or wrong.

Reviews may not affect the bottom line of a summer blockbuster, but for smaller films, they could make the difference between an awards-season goldmine and the discount bin at the video store. When the general public was still in the dark, it was critics who carried the torch for *The Hurt Locker* (2008), which became the first female-directed film to win the Oscar as Best Picture, and *Crouching Tiger, Hidden Dragon* (2000), which became the most lucrative foreign-language film of all time.

Most movies, even foolproof crowd-pleasers, are previewed for the critics in major markets. This usually happens in multiplexes padded with radio-station giveaway winners on Tuesday evenings, so the reviews can run on the opening Friday. Conscientious critics don't consult each other beforehand. (If a studio chooses not to preview a movie, as sometimes happens with horror movies or sex comedies, it's usually the sign of a stinker.)

To sweeten the deal, studios sometimes offer free trips and hotel rooms to critics and entertainment reporters whose publications permit them to go on junkets. At the junkets, the reporters get a few minutes to interview the stars, and they receive keepsakes such as baseball caps and soundtrack CDs. Ethical journalists aren't swayed by such goodies, but there are dozens of correspondents who spend every weekend at luxury hotels in Hollywood in exchange for favorable reviews.

If you've seen a lot of movie ads, you may have noticed the names in tiny type proclaiming the latest studio release "A laugh riot!" or "A nonstop thrill ride!" Your first clue that this is a freeloader is the exclamation point, which professional writers use sparingly. Your second is that you probably have never heard of the proclaimer or his vaguely identified employer. Even obscure blurbs can help a movie stand out from the pack. That's why, in 2001, Sony invented a fake critic named David Manning to provide glowing quotes for *A Knight's Tale* and *The Animal*. The studio ended up paying $1.5 million to end a class action lawsuit.

(The first time I saw one of my reviews excerpted on a DVD was on a Chinese bootleg of *Charlie and the Chocolate Factory*. It said the movie "has a nut in the middle but is not very sweet." Apparently, the packaging was assembled by a non-English speaker who assumed that my mixed review was a rave.)

In the early days of cinema, it was theater critics who were enlisted to write about the newfangled art form called motion pictures, often prompting disdain and condescension. But by the 1960s, film criticism had developed its own standards, thanks to writers such as Pauline Kael of *The New Yorker* and François Truffaut, who championed Hollywood auteurs like Alfred Hitchcock and became an influential director himself. Kael almost single-handedly rescued Warren Beatty's violent *Bonnie and Clyde* (1967) from the scrap heap of studio indifference, inaugurating a new Golden Age of American cinema.

Around that time, a new crop of university film-studies programs emerged. Attendees included young directors (Francis Ford Coppola, George Lucas) as well as aspiring critics, many of whom would go on to write for alternative weeklies like *The Village Voice*. Most big cities opened "art-house" cinemas to showcase the new and old films these critics were touting.

Robert Ebert and Gene Siskel, creators of the thumbs up/thumbs down review system, 1987. *Time & Life Pictures/Getty Images*

In the 1970s, Chicago newspaper critics Roger Ebert and Gene Siskel broadened the reach of educated criticism with their television show *Sneak Previews*. Alas, it also reduced nuanced discussions to a simple thumbs-up/thumbs-down judgment, a concession to short attention spans that is still prevalent today.

In the Internet era, anybody with a computer can be a critic. While fanboys and film scholars tend to steer readers in opposite directions, consensus sites like Rotten Tomatoes and Metacritic can offer fresh perspectives for the most important critic of all: you. ★

54

THE RATINGS SYSTEM

Do the censors need some parental guidance?

*I*t's a common complaint that Hollywood peddles sex and violence. While it's true that half of all Hollywood movies are rated R, that doesn't mean that all R-rated movies are wicked or that the raunchiest movies are the most profitable.

Although G-rated family films comprise fewer than 10 percent of movie releases, they clean up at the box office. Year after year, the list of top moneymakers includes cartoons, talking-animal flicks, and other family fare. The Pixar cartoons have been especially lucrative, averaging $250 million at the U.S. box office. Anyone with restless kids knows the value of owning these films on DVD.

When the average G-rated movie is more profitable than the average R-rated one, why is it that Hollywood doesn't make more family films? Is it because the industry is run by degenerates? Hardly. It's run by accountants who know that family films are most profitable when they're released during vacation periods and don't have to compete with each other. Flooding the market with G-rated films would water down that success rate. So on the average weekend, there is a preponderance of PG-13 and R-rated films. These are often targeted to teenagers and twenty-somethings, the largest and most coveted demographic of moviegoers.

Despite its X rating, *Midnight Cowboy* won the Academy Award for Best Picture and ranks 36 on the American Film Institute's 100 Years...100 Movies list.
© AF Archive/Alamy

For better or worse, it is undeniable that a generation with easy access to violent video games and Internet pornography is less likely to be shocked by R-rated movies than their parents and grandparents.

The current ratings system was introduced in 1968. It replaced the Hays Production Code, a simple pass/fail system that Hollywood implemented in the 1930s to burnish its bad reputation and stave off proposed state censorship laws. Under the old system, former U.S. postmaster general William H. Hays had the single-handed authority to ban films he felt were immoral.

221

Hays died in 1954, and by the 1960s, American filmmakers were fighting to reflect the changing values of the culture.

A few years after the French got a glimpse of a nude Brigitte Bardot in *And God Created Woman*, Marilyn Monroe became the first major star to film a nude scene, in 1963's *Something's Got to Give*. (Monroe died before the movie was completed.) Jayne Mansfield soon upped the ante with a topless scene in the 1963 comedy *Promises! Promises!* Four years later, the one-two punch of *Bonnie and Clyde* and *The Graduate* shattered barriers about violence and sex, respectively, in critically acclaimed hit films.

The next year, the studios and theater owners collaborated on a ratings system intended to provide parents with more guidance on what they could allow their children to see. The initial ratings under the Motion Picture Association of America, or MPAA, system were G (for general audiences), M (for mature audiences), R (for adults and accompanied minors), and X (for audiences over eighteen). In 1970, a rating called GP (subsequently changed to PG) replaced M to indicate a movie for which parental guidance was suggested.

After the X-rated 1969 movie *Midnight Cowboy*, which featured little nudity but had a hustler as a protagonist and alluded to homosexual activity, won the Academy Award for Best Picture (the only X-rated film ever to do so), pornographers co-opted the rating to add prestige to imported peep-show films like the 1967 Swedish movie *I Am Curious (Yellow)*. Eventually the X rating was replaced by NC-17. NC-17 is still generally considered a commercial kiss of death and has inaugurated several well-documented conflicts between studios and the MPAA, including for the films *Requiem for a Dream* (2000) and *Blue Valentine* (2010).

Another important change to the system was the addition of the PG-13 rating in 1984, after PG movies such as *Gremlins* and *Indiana Jones and the Temple of Doom* depicted violence that upset some parents. PG-13 is considered the minimum rating for films with drug use and non-sexual nudity.

Other criteria are harder to define. The MPAA Ratings Board is a mysterious entity comprising eight to thirteen unidentified parents who debate and vote on movies that are submitted for classification. Filmmakers are not provided with a rationale for the ratings they receive, and if they want to appeal, they have to re-edit their films and hope for the best.

In general, the Ratings Board seems more tolerant of violence than sex and more tolerant of heterosexuality than homosexuality. But the Board remains unpredictable—and arguably unnecessary and ineffective. It slapped an R rating on Mel Gibson's violent Bible story *The Passion of the Christ* in 2004, despite which the movie became the most profitable independent film of all time.

Because the ratings system is voluntary rather than legally enforceable, some filmmakers and theater chains are opting out of it, and now many art-house movies are simply labeled "not rated." ★

55

3-D

Is the eye-popping technology truly new and lucrative?

$\mathcal{T}$eenagers watching the latest superhero movie may think that 3-D is an exciting new invention, created to let them watch Green Lanterns and Autobots soar through the air. Their grandparents, on the other hand, may think it's a resurrected fad from the 1950s. But 3-D imagery is actually older than the movies.

In the nineteenth century, a device called a stereoscope was a common household amusement. It was a slide viewer with two eyeholes, through which two side-by-side images of a cityscape or natural wonder could be seen. The images merged to create an illusion of three dimensions, in a manner similar to the one still used in Viewmaster toys.

In 1915, Edwin S. Porter, who directed the pioneering movie *The Great Train Robbery* (1903), demonstrated a 3-D projection system at a theater in New York City, using two synchronized projectors that displayed color-coded images. The color-coding system, called anaglyph 3-D, was refined in the 1920s and 1930s in a handful of feature films, newsreels, and even Nazi propaganda films. But it was hard to keep the projectors perfectly synchronized, and the 3-D effect was limited.

In the 1930s, inventor Edwin S. Land of the Polaroid Corporation improved the effect by developing better polarizing filters. The outcome was demonstrated in photography exhibits and in a Chrysler ad at the 1939

New York World's Fair, but World War II delayed the technology's implementation in feature films.

Three-dimensional films finally broke out in the early 1950s. Hollywood needed novelties to compete with television, and over the course of the decade it experimented with wide-screen formats such as Cinerama and even olfactory gimmicks like Smell-O-Vision, an air-pump system developed by producer Mike Todd Jr. and his stepmother, Elizabeth Taylor. But it was 3-D that had the most immediate impact, starting with the surprise hit *Bwana Devil* (1952). A year later, *House of Wax*, starring Vincent Price, became the most successful 3-D movie yet released. The scene of a carnival barker whacking a paddle ball in the direction of the audience represented the hook that Hollywood needed. Although 3-D technology was embraced by prestige directors such as Alfred Hitchcock (in 1954's *Dial M for Murder*) and used in mainstream crowd-pleasers such as the musical *Kiss Me, Kate* (1953), it was most common in genre films, including *Creature from the Black Lagoon* (1954) and a surprising number of Westerns. The image in *Life* magazine of a movie audience gawking through cardboard glasses was as quintessentially 1950s as hula hoops and poodle skirts. By 1954 the inherent limitations of synchronized projectors had effectively ended the golden age of 3-D.

After the development of a single-projector process, the technology experienced a brief revival among the sensation-cravers of the Woodstock generation. In 1969, the low-budget 3-D skin flick *The Stewardesses* earned $27 million, the equivalent of more than $140 million today. Five years later, the potentate of pop art lent his name to *Andy Warhol's Frankenstein*, a 3-D midnight movie that was noteworthy for the forward-thrusting image of an impaled liver. Mainstream Hollywood re-embraced the technology for sequels such as *Friday the 13th Part III* (1982), *Amityville 3-D* (1983), and *Jaws 3-D* (1983).

In the new millennium, with larger and cheaper home theaters offering a viable alternative to the multiplex, theater owners have sought new inducements to get consumers to pay for movie tickets (and gas and popcorn and maybe a babysitter). The promise of a second *Star Wars* trilogy in the first decade of the 2000s convinced some exhibitors to switch to digital projectors. Then the announcement of the 3-D *Avatar*, from *Titanic* hit-maker James Cameron, convinced many to add the converters and silver screens necessary to show digital 3-D films. In 2008, the 3-D *Hannah Montana & Miley Cyrus: Best of Both Worlds Concert* paid off handsomely for early investors, and in 2009, Cameron's record-shattering *Avatar* sealed the deal for the stragglers, who shelled out as much as $100,000 per auditorium to convert their theaters.

But then a funny thing happened on the way to the pot of gold. Some 3-D movies, such as Tim Burton's *Alice in Wonderland* and the remake of

Tim Burton's 2010 film
Alice in Wonderland was
shot with conventional
two-dimensional cameras
and converted to 3-D in
post-production. © *Photos
12/Alamy*

Clash of the Titans in 2010, turned out to be conventional two-dimensional films that were retrofitted for 3-D presentation. Audiences balked at paying a surcharge for the darkened, unimpressive imagery in these hybrid films. For movies such as *Pirates of the Caribbean: On Stranger Tides*, the percentage of the American box-office booty that came from 3-D theaters was less than 50. (Overseas, 3-D remained a lucrative novelty.)

Though the autobots sequel *Transformers: Dark of the Moon*, which was filmed in 3-D by design, temporarily reversed the trend, it cost $200 million to produce, a price that few directors could afford. For theater owners who need a new gimmick, maybe it's time for Smell-O-Vision 2.0. ★

THE ACADEMY AWARDS

Does the golden boy deserve his luster?

He's more than eighty years old, only thirteen inches tall, and as fickle as the weather, but Oscar is the most coveted companion in Hollywood. The Academy Award shines brighter than any other show-business honor.

The annual Academy Awards are more than a movie contest; they're a cultural phenomenon, a celebrity summit, a fashion gala, and the most widely watched non-sports spectacle on television. Although complaining about the Oscars is nearly as popular as watching the Oscars, people in the movie business covet and respect the honor because it is awarded by their peers. The Academy of Motion Picture Arts and Sciences comprises about six thousand film professionals, and membership is by invitation only.

In most of the categories, the Oscar nominees are determined by a vote of the specialists—actors nominate actors, editors nominate editors, and so forth—while the winners are determined by a vote of the general membership. (There are arcane and ever-changing procedures for determining the documentary and foreign-film nominees, which is why they are often obscure.) All members are eligible to nominate up to five films in the Best Picture category, in priority order. Using a weighted system, a small team of ballot tabulators determines the final nominees.

In 2010, the Academy expanded the number of Best Picture finalists from five to ten, then in 2011 it announced that the number would fluctuate,

depending on how many films were listed on 10 percent of the ballots. The changes in the Best Picture category were meant to include more popular films and thus increase the television ratings, which have eroded with the rise of cable TV and the increasing visibility of the Golden Globes.

(The Globes are essentially a marketing gimmick with no credibility within the industry itself. They are awarded by an obscure organization called the Hollywood Foreign Press Association, which comprises about a hundred little-known, overseas reporters who work the junket circuit in Hollywood and are notoriously easy to bribe. The Globes' popularity may be attributed to the fact that nominations in the major categories are split into drama and comedy subsets, so twice as many movies can be touted as Golden Globe nominees in studio ads. Also, alcohol is served at the ceremony, which often makes the Globes more entertaining than other awards shows.)

There is little doubt that Golden Globe, Directors Guild, Screen Actors Guild, and Independent Spirit Award nominations can boost a movie's box office appeal, but the Academy Award confers a special status that's worth more than money.

The actual Oscar statuettes are made of a pewter-like alloy called Britannia and electroplated in copper, nickel, silver, and 24-carat gold. They weigh about 8 1/2 pounds. The design, of a nude man holding a sword and standing atop a reel of film, was created by longtime MGM art designer

Cedric Gibbons (who later won eleven Oscars, second only to Walt Disney's twenty-two).

Although there is some debate about the origin of the nickname "Oscar," the likeliest explanation is that it was coined by longtime Academy librarian Margaret Herrick, who said it looked like her uncle. Bette Davis is alleged to have made a similar claim.

As of 2011, winners' names are immediately engraved on the statuettes backstage. Since 1950, winners have been forbidden to sell or auction their trophies without first offering them to the Academy for $1; older ones are fair game. In 1999, Michael Jackson bought the Best Picture award for 1939's *Gone with the Wind* for $1.5 million, and in 2003, magician David Copperfield paid $231,000 for the statuette awarded to Michael Curtiz for directing *Casablanca*.

On the eve of the 2000 ceremony, fifty-five of the statuettes disappeared from a shipping facility in Los Angeles. A few days later, fifty-two of them were found in a trash bin in suburban Venice. The other three remain at large, as does Alice Brady's award for Best Supporting Actress for 1936's *In Old Chicago*. (Brady was home with a broken ankle, and when her name was announced, an anonymous man accepted the award on her behalf— and then fled with it.)

The world's most famous award was born during a period when Hollywood was beset by scandals and labor unrest. At the end of the silent-movie era, the Academy was created by studios and producers as a kind of industry ombudsman between studios and workers (and thus to blunt the influence of unions). The first Academy Award ceremony was a small affair held on May 16, 1929, at the Roosevelt Hotel, across Hollywood Boulevard from the cement footprints at Graumann's Chinese (and the Kodak Theater, where the Oscars are held today). The winners were announced three months in advance and the event wasn't broadcast on the radio.

In the Hollywood Golden Age of the 1930s, the Academy Awards became a more public and prestigious cultural event. By 1940, when Africa-American Hattie McDaniel accepted the Oscar as Best Supporting Actress for *Gone with the Wind*, the ceremony became an important social indicator as well. (Even though she was a nominee for her industry's highest honor, McDaniel had to sit in a segregated seating area during the award ceremony, which was picketed by civil-rights activists who decried the "Mammy" roles to which black performers were confined.)

After World War II, Hollywood celebrated what were expected to be the best years of our lives with biblical epics and Technicolor musicals, and the Academy Awards reflected that uplifted mood. Inoffensive Best Picture–winning films such as *The Greatest Show on Earth* (1952) and *Gigi* (1958) raised questions about the Academy's courage, while the religious-themed *Ben-Hur* (1959) set a record with eleven Oscars (subsequently tied by *Titanic* in 1997 and *The Lord of the Rings: Return of the King* in 2003).

In the heat of the 1960s, the old guard shared the stage with a new generation of easy-riding revolutionaries. Youth movies such as *Bonnie and Clyde* and *The Graduate*, both 1967, crashed the party with multiple nominations each, but couldn't steal the big trophy. In 1969, old-school comedian Bob Hope, who had hosted the ceremony eighteen times since 1939, was replaced as emcee and the Oscars moved to the sleek new Dorothy Chandler Pavilion in downtown Los Angeles. The 1970 ceremony, with no host, was the most-watched Oscars of all time, with 43 percent of American households tuned in to watch as the X-rated *Midnight Cowboy* was named Best Picture.

During the 1970s, the Academy Awards stage became a platform for protests. In 1971, George C. Scott refused his Best Actor award for *Patton* because he didn't believe in competing against his peers. The following year, Charlie Chaplin was given an honorary Oscar and returned to the country that had barred his re-entry twenty years earlier because of his liberal politics. The twelve-minute standing ovation the tearful comedian received was the longest in Academy Award history.

In 1973, Marlon Brando sent a Native American woman named Sacheen Littlefeather to refuse his Oscar for *The Godfather*, to protest the treatment and depiction of Native-Americans in movies and television. And five years later, accepting the Oscar for Best Supporting Actress for *Julia*, Vanessa Redgrave denounced the "Zionist hoodlums" who ran ads against the film because of her support for Palestinian statehood.

Not all of the memorable Oscar-night incidents were political. In 1974, at the height of the streaking fad, a man named Robert Opel ran naked across the stage behind presenter David Niven, prompting Niven to quip about the man's "shortcomings" (a joke that a reporter claims to have seen the actor write down before the broadcast, indicating that the whole thing was a scripted stunt).

Unscripted moments such as eleven-year-old Anna Paquin's speech-lessness (after winning Best Supporting Actress for 1993's *The Piano*) and James Cameron's declaration that he was "king of the world" (upon winning Best Director for *Titanic*) kept the Oscars a must-see TV event.

The most controversial moment in recent Oscar history was more scripted than people may realize. Four days before the 2003 Academy Awards ceremony, the United States invaded Iraq. Many Hollywood liberals were opposed to the invasion, and thousands of ordinary Americans who shared that opinion rallied in the streets of Hollywood to attract some of the attention directed at the movie awards. When the avowedly anti-war director Michael Moore won Best Documentary Feature for *Bowling for Columbine*, he invited his fellow nominees to share the stage, where he denounced the "fictitious" basis for the invasion. There was a noisy response, and ceremony producer Gil Cates cued the orchestra before Moore's allotted time had elapsed.

Backstage, where I was covering the ceremony for the *St. Louis Post-Dispatch*, Moore expressed surprise at a reporter's suggestion that he had been booed off stage. The video replays showed that virtually everyone in the auditorium had been applauding him. Many had given him a standing ovation. Subsequent acoustic analysis revealed that the catcalls came from backstage, where a few workers were gathered around an extra microphone to boo the presumptive winner Moore. In the subsequent summary of events, the pro-war cable-news networks used the amplified, off-stage audio instead of the original audio that was broadcast on ABC.

Since the attacks of September 11, 2001, the Oscar ceremony has been treated as a potential terrorist target, with beefed-up security procedures. In 2002, the ceremony moved to its new home at the Kodak Theater in the Hollywood & Highland mall (which resembles the set of D. W. Griffith's *Intolerance*, with plaster elephants looking down upon the spectacle). For several days before the ceremony, Hollywood Boulevard in front of the Kodak is closed to traffic and decorated with a wide red carpet, potted plants, and dozens of golden, man-size statues. If rain is in the forecast, the fiberglass statues are covered with clear-vinyl tarps and the entire red-carpet area is canopied.

On the day of the telecast, there are usually political and religious protesters crowded behind the sidewalk barricades alongside fans hoping to glimpse stars in the passing limousines. Those limos are subjected to checkpoints and bomb-sniffing dogs while police helicopters whir overhead.

There is a definite pecking order for the arrivals. In the morning, a few thousand pre-screened fans who applied for tickets months prior will pass through metal detectors, sit in assigned bleacher seats, and eat box lunches while they wait for the stars to arrive. In separate corrals are photographers, print reporters, and television interviewers, all of whom are required to wear formal attire. An official interviewer with an amplified microphone announces the new arrivals to the cheering crowd.

Among the first arrivals are the two accountants who tabulated the ballots. They take separate limos and separate routes to arrive at the theater carrying briefcases with duplicate sets of envelopes. (They've also memorized the winners in case the briefcases are lost or stolen.) Until the envelopes are opened, the accountants are the only people who know the names of the winners. The final tallies and second-place finishers are never revealed. (The accounting firm has verified, however, that when Barbra Streisand and Katharine Hepburn shared the award for Best Actress of 1968—for *Funny Girl* and *The Lion in Winter*, respectively—it was an absolute tie. Also, it's a myth that newcomer Marisa Tomei wasn't the intended winner for Best Supporting Actress for 1992's *My Cousin Vinny*,

and that presenter Jack Palance read the wrong name. The accountants wait in the wings and would have immediately corrected such a mistake.)

After the accountants come the directors of short, foreign, and documentary films; technical-category nominees such as sound mixer Kevin O'Connell (who has been nominated a record twenty times without winning); and celebrity chef Wolfgang Puck, who previews the meal for the post-award Governor's Ball and tosses tiny chocolate Oscars to the crowd.

The lure of the gold statue attracts the biggest stars in the world, and the sheer number of lavishly attired celebrities arriving for the ceremony becomes mind-boggling in the last few minutes before airtime. While flash bulbs illuminate the nominees, it's not unusual to see surreal groupings like Morgan Freeman, Mickey Rooney, and Miley Cyrus standing shoulder to shoulder at the bottom of the grand staircase to the Kodak Theater.

Meanwhile, the print reporters rush to a backstage annex, where we sit at long tables, view the broadcast on a closed-circuit feed, and file our stories one paragraph at a time. Sometimes a trend becomes apparent and the reporters ready a completed story based on their predictions. But the Academy skews older than the average moviegoer and more conservative than the average critic, so it is often cautious with its highest honor. In 2006, when Jack Nicholson opened the final envelope and announced that *Crash* had won Best Picture, hundreds of flustered reporters who had expected the winner to be *Brokeback Mountain* had to quickly rewrite their stories to meet midnight deadlines.

Even veteran reporters can turn into fans when a deserving honoree accepts the award and carries it backstage to answer questions. The press corps cheered for perennial also-ran Martin Scorsese when he won Best Director for *The Departed* in 2007, hailed the gender-barrier breakthrough when Kathryn Bigelow's little-seen *The Hurt Locker* beat her ex-husband James Cameron's billion-dollar *Avatar* for the directing prize in 2010, and felt protective toward pregnant Natalie Portman when she wafted into the interview room on the wings of *Black Swan* in 2011.

As soon as the ceremony ends, the job offers begin, and the winners learn that the life-changing power of the little golden man is no myth. ★

The Oscars have long inspired fashion innovation—or insanity. From left: Barbra Steisand, 1969, *photograph by Ron Galella*; Cher (later an Academy Award winner for 1987's *Moonstruck*), 1986, *photograph by Julian Wasser/Liaison*; Demi Moore, 1989, *photograph by Jim Smeal/WireImage*; Whoopi Goldberg, 1993, *photograph by Kevin Mazur/WireImage*; Björk, 2001, *photograph by Mirek Towski/FilmMagic*. *All photographs from Getty Images*

INDEX

Abyss, The, 198
Academy Awards, 229–235
Acker, Jean, 18
Actors Studio, 118
Adler, Stella, 44
Adventures of Pluto Nash, The, 65
Adventures of Superman, The, 39, 111
African Queen, 35
Airport, 134
Alamo, The, 29–30
Algonquin Hotel, 26
Alice in Wonderland, 224, 227
Aliens, 198
All About Eve, 118
Allen, Woody, 46, 52–55
Allison, Joan, 174
Ally McBeal, 58
Altobelli, Rudi, 125, 126
Ambassador Hotel, 19
American Academy of Dramatic Arts, 75
American Graffiti, 56, 192, 194
Anderson, Gilbert "Broncho Billy," 153
And God Created Woman, 222
Andy Warhol's Frankenstein, 224
Animal, The, 218
Animal House, 142
Aniston, Jennifer, 98
Annie Hall, 54
Ann Margaret, 51
Apocalypse Now, 56, 188
Arbuckle, Roscoe "Fatty," 12, 14, 18, 20–23, 81
Arkin, Alan, 65
Arlen, Harold, 165
Army Motion Picture Unit, 109
Arnaz, Desi Jr., 130
Around the World in 80 Days, 54
Artist, The, 160
Asphalt Jungle, The, 118
Astaire, Fred, 72–74
"As Time Goes By," 177
Atkins, Susan, 126, 127
Atuk, 142, 144
Autry, Gene, 29
Avatar, 167, 224, 235
Aykroyd, Dan, 142
Ayres, Lew, 74

Bacall, Lauren, 35
Baer, Max, 27
Baja Film Studios, 198
Baker, Gladys, 116
Bakley, Bonnie Lee, 45
Ball, Lucille, 171
Bancroft, Anne, 184
Barefoot in the Park, 140, 184
Baretta, 112
Bardot, Brigitte, 222
Barkleys of Broadway, The, 74
Barry, Joan, 15
Barrymore, John, 18, 27, 160
Barrymore, Lionel, 180
Batman, 182
Baum, L. Frank, 161
Beatty, Warren, 52, 120, 133, 140, 182, 218
Beau Brummel, 18
Beausoleil, Bobby, 126
Bello, Marino, 24, 26
Belmondo, Jean-Paul, 132
Belushi, John, 142–145
Benchley, Peter, 191

Ben-Hur, 86, 231–232
Benigni, Roberto, 48
Bennett, Murray, 174
Bergman, Ingrid, 175, 177
Bergen, Candace, 184
Berle, Milton, 48
Bern, Paul, 24, 111
Berry, Dennis, 134
Bertrand, Marcheline, 98
Beverly Hillbillies, The, 126, 163
Beverly Hills Cop, 63
Bigelow, Kathryn, 235
Big Trail, The, 28
Biograph Company, 155
The Birth of a Nation, 154–157
Black Panthers, 134
Black Swan, 235
Blake, Robert, 45, 112
Blanchett, Cate, 148
Blood and Sand, 18
Blues Brothers, The, 142, 143
Blue Valentine, 222
Bob & Carol & Ted & Alice, 140
Bogart, Humphrey, 32–35, 66, 86, 102, 175
Bogdanovich, Peter, 15
Bolger, Ray, 163, 164
Bonjour Tristesse, 132
Bonnie and Clyde, 140, 182, 187, 218, 222
Borgnine, Ernest, 187, 188
Born on the Fourth of July, 68
Bow, Clara, 12, 28
Bowling for Columbine, 232
The Boys in the Band, 146
Brady, Alice, 231
Brady, Matthew, 22, 23
"Brain Damage," 166
Brainstorm, 140
Brando, Cheyenne, 44
Brando, Christian, 40, 44, 45
Brando, Christian Shannon, 45
Brando, Marlon, 36, 39, 40–45, 49, 105, 108, 187, 188, 232
Braudy, Leo, 104
Breathless, 132
Brecht, Bertolt, 35
Bridesmaids, 216
Bringing Up Baby, 83
Brody, Sam, 137
Brokeback Mountain, 146, 148, 235
Brooks, Louise, 15
Brooks, Mel, 184
Brown, Jerry, 140
Brynner, Yul, 128
Bullitt, 51
Burke, Billie, 102
Burton, Richard, 39, 90–95, 127
Bus Stop, 118–119, 137
BUtterfield 8, 92
Bwana Devil, 224

Caan, James, 188
Cabinet of Dr. Caligari, The, 175
Cagney, James, 34, 66
Cameron, James, 196–198, 224, 232, 235
Campbell, Joseph, 194
Candy, 148
Candy, John, 142, 144
Cannon, Dyan, 83
Capote, 148
Capra, Frank, 178, 180, 181

Captain America: The First Avenger, 29, 216
Captains Courageous, 77
Carefree, 74
Carol Burnett Show, The, M>, 87
Carpenter, Harlean, 24
Carroll, Tod, 144, 145
Carson, Kit, 153
Casablanca, 51, 66, 174–177, 231
Catch-22, 184
Cates, Gil, 233
Cat on a Hot Tin Roof, 140
Cat's Meow, The, 15
Centaur Studio, 203
Central Casting, 24
Change of Habit, A, 51
Changeling, 99
Chaplin, Charlie, 12–15, 18, 20, 82, 160, 231
Chaplin, Geraldine, 15
Charisse, Cyd, 74
Chase, Chevy, 142
Cher, 234
Cherrill, Virginia, 82
Chicago Tribune, 18–19
Church of Scientology, 68–69
Cimber, Matt, 137
Circus, The, 14
Citizen Kane, 29, 171–173, 185, 203
City Lights, 14, 82, 160
Clansman, The, 155
Clash of the Titans, 228
Clean and Sober, 145
Cleopatra, 92, 203
Clift, Ethel "Sunny," 36
Clift, Montgomery, 36–39, 86, 92, 108
Close Encounters of the Third Kind, 189
Cocktail, 68
Cohn, Harry, 118
Coleman, Gary, 62
Colombo, Joe, 188
Columbo, 191
Color of Money, The, 68
Columbia Pictures, 118, 203
Coming Home, 98
Committee for the First Amendment, 35
Confederacy of Dunces, A, 145
Conklin, Chester, 12
Connery, Sean, 133
Conqueror, The, 30
Conrad, Joseph, 171
Conversation, The, 56
Cool World, 98
Copperfield, David, 231
Coppola, Carmine, 188
Coppola, Francis Ford, 68, 185–188, 194, 218
Corrigan, Thomas, 113
Counterattack, 35
Coward, Noel, 86, 94
Cox, Wally, 44
Crane, Fred, 109, 111
Crash, 148, 235
Crosby, Bing, 79–81, 116
Crouching Tiger, Hidden Dragon, 217
Crowe, Bernard, 126
Cruise, Tom, 66–69, 98
Cruising, 146
Cukor, George, 83, 84
Cummings, Robert, 102
Curious Case of Benjamin Button, The, 99
Curtis, Tony, 113
Curtiz, Michael, 51, 175, 231

Daddy Day Care, 65
Dallas, 98
Daniels, Anthony, 192
Darby, Kim, 184
Darin, Bobby, 48
Dark Knight, The, 148, 149
Dark Side of the Moon, The, 161, 165
Davern, Dennis, 141
Davidson, Bill, 78
Davies, Marion, 15, 173
Davis, Bette, 94, 103, 231
Davis, Gray, 61
Day, Doris, 87, 184
Days of Thunder, 68
Day the Clown Cried, The, 46, 47–48
Dead Heat on a Merry-Go-Round, 56
Deadly Illusions, 27
Dean, James, 36, 105–108, 130, 138
Defiant Ones, The, 113
De Forest, Lee, 158
De Havilland, Olivia, 175
DeKova, Frank, 187
de Lara, Marquesa, 19
Delmont, Bambina Maude, 22
DeMille, Cecil B., 113, 230
Dempsey, Jack, 19
De Niro, Robert, 144, 188
Denslow, W. W., 161
Denton, Charles, 48
De Palma, Brian, 194
Departed, The, 235
Depp, Johnny, 108, 149
DeVito, Danny, 62
DeWilde, Brandon, 130
DGA Lifetime Achievement Award, 157
DiCaprio, Leonardo, 197
Dickson, William K. L., 152, 158
DiMaggio, Joe, 116, 118, 119, 120
DiMaggio, Joe Jr., 120
Dinner at Eight, 173
Director's Guild of America, 157
Dirty Harry, 51
Disney, Walt, 34, 163
Dixon, Thomas Jr., 155
Dmytryk, Edward, 39
Don Juan, 160
Doork, Helmut, 48
Dougherty, James, 118
Drake, Betsy, 83
Drake, Nick, 149
Dreamgirls, 65
Dream Street, 160
Dreyfuss, Richard, 191
Dr. Doolittle, 65
Dr. Doolittle (musical), 194
Dr. Strangelove, 51
Drollet, Dag, 44, 45
Duel, 191
Dunaway, Faye, 140
Dunne, Irene, 104
duPont, Mariana, 83
Durfee, Minta, 20
Duvall, Robert, 188
D. W. Griffith Award, 157
Dylan, Bob, 108, 148

East of Eden, 105, 108
Eastwood, Clint, 15, 128, 130
Ebert, Roger, 185, 218
Ebsen, Buddy, 163

Eddie Murphy Delirious, 63
Eddie Murphy Raw, 63
Edison, Thomas, 152, 158, 202
Edison Company, 158
Empire Strikes Back, The, 194
Endless Love, 68
Enron Corporation, 61
Entwistle, Peg, 102–104
E.T., 169
Étaix, Pierre, 47
Evans, Robert, 188
Everybody Comes to Rick's, 174
Exodus, 130

Fairbanks, Douglas, 12, 18
Fairmount Historical Museum, 108
Family Affair, 104
Famous Players-Lasky Corporation, 18
Farley, Chris, 142, 145
Farrell, Colin, 149
Farrow, John, 54
Farrow, Mia, 52, 54–55
Father of the Bride, 90
Fellini, Federico, 92
Ferrell, Will, 145
Field Photographic Unit, 29
Fields, W. C., 163
Fincher, David, 98
Fine Madness, A, 133
Firelight, 189
Fischbach, Fred, 22
Fisher, Carrie, 193, 194
Fisher, Eddie, 92
500 Club, 47
Fleming, Victor, 165
Flockhart, Calista, 58
Fly Away Home, 36
Flying Down to Rio, 74
Folger, Abigail, 127
Follow the Fleet, 74
Fonda, Henry, 29, 35, 44
Fonda, Jane, 140
Ford, Harrison, 56–58, 193, 194
Ford, John, 29, 34, 78
Formula, The, 40
Fortensky, Larry, 95
Fortune and Men's Eyes, 130
48 Hours, 63
Four Feathers, The, 146
Four Horsemen of the Apocalypse, The, 18
Fox Films Corporation, 34
Fox Studios, 119, 203
Foy, Eddie Sr., 74
Frankenstein, 86
Freedom of Information Act, 134
Freshman, The, 44
Freud, 39
From Here to Eternity, 38, 111, 140, 141
F-Troop, 187
Frykowski, Wojciech, 127
Fugitive, The, 58
Funny Girl, 233

Gable, Clark, 26, 27, 118, 119
Gang That Couldn't Shoot Straight, The, 188
Garbo, Greta, 27
Gardner, Ava, 184
Garland, Judy, 163, 164
Garfield, John, 35
Garretson, William, 126
Gary, Romain, 134
Gates, Darryl, 120
Gates, Phyllis, 38, 87
Gay Divorce, The, 74
General Tire and Rubber Company, 203
Gershwin, George, 72, 74

Gershwin, Ira, 74
Getting Straight, 56
Giancana, Sam, 119, 120, 123
Giant, 38, 105, 108, 130
G.I. Blues, 51
Gibbons, Cedric, 231
Gibson, Hoot, 160
Gibson, Mel, 222
Giffords, Stanley, 118
Gigi, 54, 231
Gilbert, John, 12
Gielgud, John, 132
Gilliam, Gerry, 148, 149
Girl Can't Help It, The, 135, 137
Girl Crazy, 74
Girl, Interrupted, 98
Gish, Lillian, 102
Glory Days, 98
Godard, Jean-Luc, 132
Godard, Paulette, 15
Godfather, The, 44, 185–188, 232
Godfather Part II, The, 185, 188
Goddess, 120
Going My Way, 81, 113
Goldberg, Whoopi, 234
Golden Globes, 230
Gold Diggers of 1933, 74
Gomer Pyle, 86
Gone with the Wind, 109, 111, 165, 167–170, 194, 216, 231
Goodrich, William, 23
Goodbye, Mr. Chips, 169
Goodbye Natalie, Goodbye Splendour, 141
Gordon, Flash, 192
Gould, Deborah, 121
Governator, The, 62
Graduate, The, 66, 140, 182–184, 222
Grand Hotel, 27
Grant, Cary, 78, 82–85
Great Depression, 15
Great Dictator, The, 14, 15
Greatest Gift, The, 178
Greatest Show on Earth, The, 231
Great Race, The, 14
Great Train Robbery, The, 152–153, 223
Greed, 46
Green Berets, The, 30
Greene, Graham, 132
Green Promise, The, 140
Greenson, Ralph, 120–121
Greenstreet, Sydney, 175
Gregson, Richard, 140
Griffith, D. W., 14, 18, 154, 155, 157, 160, 233
Grodin, Charles, 184
Grogan, Clem, 127
Guess Who's Coming to Dinner, 78
Guinness, Alec, 105
Gunsmoke, 56
Guys and Dolls, 42, 43, 44
Gyllenhaal, Jake, 146, 148
Gypsy, 140

Haber, Joyce, 134
Hackman, Gene, 184
Haley, Jack, 163, 164
Hal Roach Studios, 24, 112
Hamel, Veronica, 119
Hamill, Mark, 194
Hamilton, Margaret, 163
Hamilton, Murray, 184
Hamlet, 94
Hammett, Dashiell, 35
Hannah and Her Sisters, 54
Hannah Montana & Miley Cyrus: Best of Both Worlds Concert, 224
Harburg, E. Y., 165

Hargitay, Mickey, 61, 137
Hargitay, Mariska, 137
Harlow, Jean, 24–27, 111, 118
Harris, Barbara, 83
Harris, Mildred, 15
Harry Potter, 66
Hart, Buddy, 58
Hart, John, 58
Hartman, Phil, 145
Hart, S., William, 12, 14
Hart to Hart, 140
Hasni, Ahmed, 134
Hawn, Goldie, 191
Haworth, Jill, 130
Hayden, Tom, 149
Hays Production Code, 221
Hays, Susan, 94
Hays, William H., 23, 160, 221–222
Hearst, William Randolph, 15, 22, 173
Heartbreak Kid, The, 184
Heart of Darkness, 171
Heiress, The, 38
Held, Richard, 134
Hell's Angels, 26
Help, The, 216
"Helter Skelter," 126
Hemingway, Mariel, 54
Hendrix, Jimi, 137
Henreid, Paul, 175
Hendry, Whitey, 27
Hepburn, Katharine, 39, 75–78, 83, 84, 233
Herrick, Margaret, 231
Hercules in New York, 61
Hershey, Barbara, 184
Heston, Charlton, 130
Hewitt, Raymond, 134
Hickman, Bill, 106
Hidden Fortress, The, 194
High and the Mighty, The, 113
High Sierra, 34
Hilton, Nicky, 92
Hinman, Gary, 126
Hitchcock, Alfred, 46, 83
Hitler, Adolf, 15, 47–48
Hoffa, Jimmy, 119
Hoffman, Dustin, 66, 140, 182
Hoffman, Philip Seymour, 148
Hollingshead, Richard, 208
Hollywood and Vine, 203
Holmes, Katie, 69
Hollywoodland, 111
Hollywood Memorial Park Cemetery, 19, 113
Hollywood Squares, 44
Hollywood Ten, 35
Holy Man, 65
Hood, Darla, 114
Hoover, J. Edgar, 14–15, 119, 120, 134
Hope, Bob, 52, 79–81, 230
Hopper, Dennis, 130, 138
Horse Feathers, 173
Hot Saturday, 82, 83
Houseman, John, 171, 173
House of Un-American Activities Committee, 15. 34
House of Wax, 224
Howard, Leslie, 34
Howard, "Stooge" Shemp, 23
Hubbard, L. Ron, 69
Hudson, Rock, 38, 86–88
Hughes, Howard, 26, 78, 83, 171, 203
Hunter, Tab, 87
Hunt, Susan, 94
Hurt Locker, The, 217, 235
Huston, John, 34, 35, 39, 94
Hutton, Barbara, 83
Hyde, Johnny, 118

I Am Curious (Yellow), 222
Ibanez, Vicente Blasco, 18
Ibsen, Henrik, 103
Imaginarium of Doctor Parnassus, The, 148
I'm Not There, 148
Ince, Thomas, 15
Incomparable Atuk, The, 144
Indiana Jones and the Last Crusade, 57
Industrial Light & Magic, 195
In Old Chicago, 231
Interview with the Vampire, 98
Inside Daisy Clover, 140
In the Land of Blood and Honey, 99
Intolerance, 157, 233
Issa, Darrell, 61, 62
It Happened One Night, 180
It's a Wonderful Life, 113, 165, 178–181
It Takes a Thief, 140

Jack and the Beanstalk, 153
Jackson, Michael, 231
Jailhouse Rock, 49
James Dean Festival, 108
Jaws, 189–191
Jayne Mansfield Story, The, 61
The Jazz Singer, 158–160
J. Edgar, 15
"Jitterbug, The" 165
John Birch Society, 29
Johnny Suede, 98
Johnson, Don, 130
Jolie, Angelina, 96–99
Jolie-Pitt Foundation, 99
Jolson, Al, 16, 158, 160
Jones, Carolyn, 51
Jones, Tom, 127
Judgment at Nuremberg, 39
Julia, 232
Julius Caesar, 44

Kael, Pauline, 218
Kasabian, Linda, 126
Kashfi, Anna, 44
Katt, William, 194
Kaye, Danny, 35
Kazan, Elia, 35, 140–141, 188
Keaton, Buster, 12, 23
Keaton, Diane, 54
Keith, Robert, 104
Keith, Brian, 104
Kelly, Emmett, 48
Kelly, Gene, 35
Kelly, Jack, 82
Kennedy, John F., 61, 116, 119, 123
Kennedy, Robert, 116, 119–120, 121, 123, 130, 134
Kenner Products, 194
Kerr, Deborah, 132
Keystone Kops, 12, 14, 20
Khan, Genghis, 30
Khrushchev, Nikita, 29
Kid Creole, 49
Kidman, Nicole, 66, 68
King and I, The, 128
King Kong, 203
King, Martin Luther Jr., 134
King of Comedy, The, 48
Kinison, Sam, 142, 144
Kirkwood, James Jr., 130
Kitty Foyle, 74
K-19: The Widowmaker, 58
Knight's Tale, A, 146, 218
Krenwinkel, Patricia, 126, 127
Kubrick, Stanley, 44
Kung-Fu, 56
Kurosawa, Akira, 194

Ladd, Alan, 66, 192
Ladies of the Chorus, 118
La Dolce Vita, 92, 94
Lahr, Bert, 164
Lamour, Dorothy, 79
Lancaster, Burt, 38
Land, Edwin S., 223
Lara Croft: Tomb Raider, 98
Larson, Jack, 39
Last Stand, The, 62
Last Tango in Paris, 40
Lauer, Matt, 68
Laurel & Hardy, 24, 112
Law and Order: Special Victims Unit, 137
Lawford, Peter, 119, 121
Law, Jude, 149
Leave It to Beaver, 56, 58
Ledger, Heath, 146–149
Lee, Ang, 146
Lee, Gypsy Rose, 35
Leigh, Vivien, 109
Lemmon, Leonore, 111
Lennon, John, 108, 130
Leone, Sergio, 187
Less Than Zero, 98
Letterman, David, 58
Lewis, Juliette, 98
Lewis, Jerry, 46–48, 65
Liberty Films, 180
Life Is Beautiful, 146
Life magazine, 82, 118
Life of an American Fireman, 153
Lightfoot, Gordon, 144
Lights of New York, 160
Lilith, 133
Limelight, 15
Lindbergh, Charles, 160
Lion in the Winter, The, 233
Little Champ, 12–15
Littlefeather, Sacheen, 44, 188, 232
Little Miss Sunshine, 65
Little Rascals, 113
Lloyd, Harold, 12
LoBianca, Leno, 127
LoBianca, Rosemary, 127
Lombard, Carole, 27
Lone Ranger, The, 58
Long Goodbye, The, 61
Look magazine, 118
Lord of the Rings, The, 232
Loren, Sophia, 137
Los Angeles Times, 134
Losin' It, 68
Love, American Style, 56
Love Happy, 118
Love Me Tender, 49
Lover Come Back, 87
Love with the Proper Stranger, 140
Loving You, 49
Loy, Myrna, 104
Lubitch, Ernst, 46
LucasArts, 195
Lucas, George, 187, 191, 192–195, 218
Luv, 56

Mad Hopes, The, 102
Magnificent Ambersons, The, 46
Making Love, 186
Maltese Falcon, The, 34, 175
Manchester, William, 29
Manhattan, 54
Mankiewicz, Ben, 173
Mankiewicz, Herman, 171–173
Mankiewicz, Joseph L., 92
Manning, David, 218
Mannix, Eddie, 111

Mannix, Toni, 111
Man's Castle, A, 77
Mansfield, Jayne, 135–137, 222
Mansfield, Paul, 135
Manson, Charles, 124–127
Man Who Laughs, The, 175
Marcus Welby, M.D., 191
Marley, John, 187
Martin, Dean, 39, 47
Marty, 187
Marx Brothers, 52, 118
Marx, Samuel, 27
"Mary Had a Little Lamb," 152
Mason, James, 94
Master and Commander, 198
Matthau, Walter, 51
Mayer, Louis B., 27, 155, 163
May, Elaine, 184
Mayhew, Peter, 193
McCarthy, Kevin, 38
McCartney, Paul, 166
McDaniel, Hattie, 231
McFarland, George, 114
McGrew, Charles, 24
McHale's Navy, 187
McMillan & Wife, 87
McQueen, Steve, 140
Meet Dave, 65
Melcher, Terry, 125, 126
Méliès, Georges, 152–153
Men, The, 44
Menken, Helen, 34
Meredith, Burgess, 35
Methot, Mayo, 34
MGM, 26, 27
Michael's Pub, 54
Midnight Cowboy, 221, 222, 232
Midnight in Paris, 55
Miller, Ann, 74
Miller, Arthur, 35, 116, 118–119
Miller, Jonny Lee, 98
Millette, Dorothy, 26, 27
Mineo, Sal, 128–131
Minority Report, 66
Miracle on 34th Street, 138
Misfits, The, 39, 119
Mission Impossible: Ghost Protocol, 69
Mission: Impossible, 68
Mix, Tom, 12
Modern Times, 14, 160
Mod Squad, The, 56
Moneyball, 99
Monkees, The, 125
Monkey Business, 173
Monroe, Marilyn, 39, 116–123, 135, 222
Monster's Ball, 146
Moore, Demi, 235
Moore, Mary Tyler, 51
Moore, Michael, 232–233
Moreuil, François, 133
Morgan, Frank, 163
Mostel, Zero, 35
Motion Picture Association of America, 160, 222
Mountain Eagle, The, 46
Mr. Junior Europe, 59
Mr. & Mrs. Smith, 98
Mr. Olympia, 61
Mr. Peepers, 44
Mr. Smith Goes to Washington, 169
Mr. Universe, 59, 61
Mulholland Drive, 38, 45
Muni, Paul, 34
Murnau, F. W., 160
Murphy, Eddie, 62, 63–65
Murray, Bill, 142
Murray, Eunice, 120, 121

Murray, Lita, 15
Musso & Frank Grill, 45
Mutiny on the Bounty, 44
My Cousin Vinny, 235
My Big Fat Greek Wedding, 216
My Favorite Wife, 83

Nabors, Jim, 86–88
Nader, Saladin, 127
National Geographic, 106
National Lampoon Lemmings, 142
National Velvet, 90
Navarra, Carlos, 134
Ned Kelly, 146
Needles, Ellanora, 109
Negri, Pola, 15, 19
Nelkin, Stacey, 54
Newman, Paul, 108, 130
News of the World, 99
Newsweek, 134
New Yorker, The, 218
New York Evening Journal, 19
New York Times, 36, 173
Nichols, Mike, 94, 182, 184
Nicholson, Jack, 235
Night and Day, 83
Night Gallery, 191
Night of the Iguana, 94
Night to Remember, A, 198
Nissen, Greta, 26
Niven, David, 132, 232
Nixon, Richard, 34
Noguchi, Thomas, 121
Nolan, Christopher, 148
Nolte, Nick, 63, 194
Norbit, 65
Nutty Professor, The, 47
Nutty Professor, The (1996), 63, 65

O'Brien, Joan, 48
Ocean's Eleven, 98
O'Connell, Kevin, 235
Of Mice and Men, 169
Olivier, Laurence, 187
Olsen, Jimmy, 39
Olsen, Mary-Kate, 148
O'Neal, Ryan, 188
O'Neill, Eugene, 15
One-Eyed Jacks, 44
On the Waterfront, 40
Opel, Robert, 232
O'Sullivan, Maureen, 54
Otash, Fred, 121
Other Side of Midnight, The, 194
O'Toole, Peter, 52, 94
Ott, Fred, 152
Our Gang, 112, 113
Outsiders, The, 68

Pacino, Al, 188
Paint Your Wagon, 134
Palance, Jack, 235
Pallete, Pilar, 29
Paltrow, Gwyneth, 98
Pan, Hermes, 74
Paradise, Hollywood Style, 51
Paramount, 20, 69, 185, 187, 188, 202, 203
Parent, Steven, 126
Parent Trap, 104
Paris Exposition, 158
Parker, Dorothy, 35, 180
Parker, Tom, 51
Pasadena Playhouse, 109
Passion of the Christ, The, 22
Pat and Mike, 113
Patriot, The, 46, 146

Patton, 187, 231
Paul Whiteman Orchestra, 79
Penn, Arthur, 187
People magazine, 98, 99
Perkins, Anthony, 87
Perry, Tyler, 216
Petrified Forest, The, 34
Peyton Place, 54
Philadelphia Story, The, 77, 86
Phillips Andover, 32
Philips, Mary, 34
Photoplay, 35
Pickford, Mary, 12, 18, 230
Pieces of My Heart: A Life, 141
Pillow Talk, 87
Pink Floyd, 161, 165, 166
Piott, Jack, 113
Pitt, Brad, 96–99
Place in the Sun, A, 38, 92
Planet of the Apes, 198
Playboy magazine, 30, 118
Plaza Hotel, 26
Plymouth Adventure, The, 78
Points West, 160
Poitier, Sidney, 113
Polanski, Roman, 125, 126, 127
Porter, Cole, 86
Porter, Edwin S., 153, 224
Portman, Natalie, 235
Portnoy's Complaint, 185
Potter, Phyllis, 72
Powell, Eleanor, 74
Powell, William, 27
Power of Myth, The, 194
Preminger, Otto, 130, 132
Presley, Elvis, 49–51, 63, 108, 138
Presley, Lisa Marie, 51
Previn, Andre, 52, 54
Previn, Soon-Yi, 52, 53, 54–55
Price, Vincent, 224
Private Lives, 94
Private War of Major Benson, The, 130
Producers, The, 184
Promises! Promises!, 137, 222
Proulx, Annie, 146
P.S. Your Cat Is Dead, 130
Puck, Wolfgang, 31
Purple Rise of Cairo, The, 54
Puzo, Mario, 185

Quinn, Anthony, 187

Radcliffe, Daniel, 66
Radner, Gilda, 142
Raft, George, 34, 175
Raiders of the Lost Ark, 191
Rain Man, 68
Rains, Claude, 175
Raintree County, 38, 39, 92
Rambova, Natacha, 18
Rappe, Virginia, 22
Ratner, Brett, 65
Rat Pack, 47, 119
Ray, Nicholas, 130, 138
Reagan, Nancy, 61
Reagan, Ronald, 61, 108, 174, 175, 184
Rebel Without a Cause, 51, 105, 106, 108, 130, 138
Red Channels, 35
Red Dust, 26, 27
Redford, Robert, 98, 140, 182, 188
Redgrave, Vanessa, 232
Red-Headed Woman, 26
Red River, 36
Red Scare, 29, 34
Reed, Donna, 38, 113, 180
Reeves, George, 109–111

Reeves, Steve, 59
Reflections in the Golden Eye, 39
Reid, Wallace, 23
Republic Pictures, 29
Requiem for a Dream, 222
Reynolds, Debbie, 92
Richards, Keith, 144
Richler, Mordecai, 144
Riefenstahl, Leni, 154
Ringo Kid, the, 29
Rin Tin Tin, 12
Risky Business, 68
River of No Return, 122, 123
River Runs Through It, A, 98
RKO Pictures, 72, 104, 171, 173, 178, 203
Roach, Hal, 112
"Road" comedies, 79, 81
Roberta, 74
Robinson, Edward G., 34, 35, 187
Rogers, Ginger, 72–74
Rogers, John, 74
Rogers, Mimi, 68
Rogers, Will, 112
Rosemary's Baby, 54
Rose Tattoo, The, 128
Ross, Katharine, 184
Rosson, Harold, 27
Roth, Philip, 185
Roth, Sanford, 106
Roy Rogers Show, The, 113
Rudolph Valentino Medal, 18
R.U.R., 75

Saint Joan, 132, 133
Sakall, S. Z. "Cuddles," 175
Sands of Iwo Jima, The, 29
"San Fernando Valley, The," 81
San Francisco Examiner, 22
Saratoga, 27
Saturday Night Live, 63, 142
Schneider, Maria, 40
Schulberg, Budd, 35
Schwarzenegger, Arnold, 59–62
Scorsese, Martin, 235
Scott, George C., 187, 231
Scott, Randolph, 82–85
Search, The, 38
Searchers, The, 138
Seberg, Jean, 132–134
Sebring, Jay, 126
Sellers, Peter, 65
Selznick, David O. 72, 74, 104, 175
Send Me No Flowers, 87
Sennett, Mack, 12, 20
September, 46
Se7en, 98
Seven Year Itch, The, 118
Sex and the Single Girl, 140
Sexiest Man Alive, 98
Shaffner, Franklin, 187
Shagan, Steve, 40
Shall We Dance, 74
Shane, 38, 130
Shaw, George Bernard, 103, 132
Shaw, Robert, 190
Shawshank Redemption, The, 185
Shearer, Harry, 47, 48
She Done Him Wrong, 83
Sheen, Martin, 108
Sheik, The, 18
Sheridan, Anne, 174
Sherman, Lowell, 22
She Wore a Yellow Ribbon, 29
Shields, Brooke, 68
Shire, Talia, 188
Shrek, 65

Shriver, Maria, 61
Shuster, Joe, 111
Siegel, Jerry, 111
Sinatra, Frank, 38, 43, 47, 54, 119, 123, 127 , 187
Singin' in the Rain, 160
Sirhan Sirhan, 130
Sirk, Douglas, 87
Siskel, Gene, 218
Six Bridges to Cross, 128
68 Comeback Special, 49
Smiler with the Knife, The, 171
Smith, Cathy Evelyn, 144
Smith, Ludlow Ogden, 78
Sneak Previews, 218
Snow White and the Seven Dwarfs, 27, 154, 163, 169
Soderbergh, Steven, 98
Somebody Up There Likes Me, 108, 130
Some Like It Hot, 119
Something's Got to Give, 119, 222
"Somewhere Over the Rainbow," 165
Sondergaard, Gale, 163
So Proudly We Hail, 109
Sound of Music, The, 167, 169, 216
Splendor in the Grass, 140
Splendour, 140
Spacek, Sissy, 194
Spielberg, Steven, 149, 189–191
Spy magazine, 47, 48
Stagecoach, 29, 169
Stallone, Sylvester, 61
Star Is Born, A, 51
Star Wars, 51, 56, 167, 191, 192–195, 224
Stay Hungry, 61
Steinbeck, John, 137
Steiner, Max, 177
Sterling, Ford, 12
Stewardesses, The, 224
Stewart, James, 29, 113, 178, 181
St. Francis Hotel, 22
Stillman, Patricia, 83
Stiltz, Bud, 113
Stone, Oliver, 68
Streetcar Named Desire, A, 44
Streisand, Barbra, 51, 233, 234
Suddenly, Last Summer, 39
Sugarland Express, The, 191
Summers, Anthony, 120
Sunday, Billy, 22
Sunday Bloody Sunday, 146
"Sundown," 144
Sun Records, 49
Sunrise, 160
Sunset Boulevard, 38
Superman and the Mole Men, 111
Swing Time, 72, 73, 74
Switch, 140
Switzer, Carl, 112–113, 114
Sylvia Scarlett, 83

Taps, 68
Tarzan, 54
Tate, Sharon, 124–127
Taub, Mae, 22
Taylor, Elizabeth, 38, 87, 90–95, 127, 184, 224
Taylor, William Desmond, 23
Tea and Sympathy, 86
Temple, Shirley, 163
Ten Commandments, The, 113, 167
10 Things I Hate About You, 146
Teriipia, Tarita, 44
Terminator, The, 61, 62, 198
Thalberg, Irving, 27
Theatre Guild, 103
Thelma & Louise, 98
They're Coming to Get Me, 160

13 Women, 104
This Property Is Condemned, 140
Thomas, Danny, 187
Thornton, Billy Bob, 98
Thousand Words, A, 65
THX, 195
THX-1138, 187, 192
Tierney, Gene, 78
Titanic, 167, 169, 196–198, 216, 232
Today Show, The, 68
Todd, Michael, 92
ToTodd, Mike Jr., 224
Toland, Gregg, 173
Tolson, Clyde, 15
Tomei, Marisa, 233, 235
Tonight Show, The, 61–62
Toole, John Kennedy, 145
Top Gun, 68
Top Hat, 74
Tower Heist, 65
Tracy, John, 77
Tracy, Spencer, 34, 39, 75–78
Trading Places, 63
Transformers, 167, 228
Travers, Henry, 102
Treadwell, Louise, 75, 76, 77
Trip to the Moon, A, 153
Triumph of the Will, 154
True Grit, 30, 51
Truffaut, Francois, 218
Turnupseed, Donald, 106
Twelve Monkeys, 98
20th Century Fox, 118, 192, 198
Twilight, 167
Twins, 62
"2000 Pound Bee, The" 144

United Artists, 14, 18, 192
Universal Studios, 189, 203
Up the River, 34

Valentino, Rudolph, 12, 16–19
Valley of the Dolls, The, 126
Van Doren, Mamie, 137
Van Doren Stern, Philip, 178
Van Houten, Leslie, 127
Veidt, Conrad, 175
Ventures, The, 144
Via Veneto, 94
Viva Las Vegas, 51
Voight, Jon, 98
von Stroheim, Erich, 46

Wachsberger, Nat, 48
Wagner, 94
Wagner, Robert, 138, 140, 141
Walken, Christopher, 140, 141, 194
Wallace, Bill "Superfoot," 144
Wallis, Hal, 51, 174
Walsh, Raoul, 28
Wanted, 99
Ward, Burt, 182
War Department, 29
Warhol, Andy, 39
Warner Bros., 23, 34, 109, 160, 174, 175, 203
Warner, John, 94
War of the Worlds, The, 171
Watson, Charles, 125, 126–127
Watson, Emma, 66
Wayne, John, 28–30, 36, 51
Wayward Bus, The, 137
Webb, Charles, 182
Weissmuller, Johnny, 54
Welles, Orson, 29, 35, 46, 171–173
"We're in the Money," 74
West, Mae, 83

West Side Story, 51, 138
Westwood Village Memorial Park, 141
Whale, James, 86
What's New Pussycat?, 52
"White Christmas," 79
"White Pants Willie," 32
Who's Afraid of Virginia Woolf?, 94, 184
Wilcox, Daeida, 202
Wilcox, Harvey, 202
Wild Duck, The, 103
Wilder, Billy, 119
Wilder, Thornton, 36
Wilding, Michael, 38, 92
Williams, John, 191
Williams, Lionel, 131
Williams, Michelle, 148
Williams, Robin, 144
Williams, Sybil, 92
Williams, Tennessee, 36, 44, 94, 128
Williams, Theresa, 131
Willson, Henry, 87
Will Success Spoil Rock Hunter?, 135
Wilson, Dennis, 125
Wilson, Dooley, 175
Wilson, Woodrow, 155
Winfrey, Oprah, 69, 195
Wired: The Short Life and Fast Times of John Belushi, 144
Witness, 56
Wizard of Oz, The, 102, 161–166, 169, 173
Woman of the Year, 77
Wonderful Wizard of Oz, The, 161
Wood, Lana, 141
Wood, Natalie, 120, 130, 138–141
Wood, Ron, 144
Woodward, Bob, 144
Written on the Wind, 87
Wütherich, Rolf, 105
Wuthering Heights, 169

X-Men, 198

Yank magazine, 118
You Don't Mess with the Zohan, 167
Young Lions, The, 39
Young, Gig, 105
Young, Loretta, 77

Zabriskie Point, 56
Zanuck, Darryl F., 163
Zelig, 54
Zwillman, Abner "Longie," 26

ABOUT THE AUTHOR

*J*oe Williams is the film critic for the daily *St. Louis Post-Dispatch* and the website stltoday.com. Previously he worked as a movie extra, set painter, and rock critic in Hollywood. He lives in a historic all-metal Lustron home in suburban St. Louis, Missouri, drives a 1966 Plymouth Fury, and spends his free time at drive-in movie theaters. His previous book was *Entertainment on the Net.* ★

ACKNOWLEDGMENTS

*I*n accepting this award for Luckiest Author, I have many people to thank while the rest of you can go get popcorn.

I am grateful to the good people at the Voyageur Press, particularly Grace Labatt and Dennis Pernu, and to Daniel Durchholz for arranging the introduction.

My past and present colleagues at the *St. Louis Post-Dispatch*—including Arnie Robbins, Jody Mitori, Calvin Wilson, Kevin Johnson, Joe Holleman, Gail Pennington, Diane Keaggy, Ray Mark Rinaldi, Ellen Futterman, Harper Barnes, Joe Pollack, David Bonetti, Christine Bertelson, and Paul Hampel—have ensured that I have the best day job a boy could wish for.

Like many in my profession, I am indebted to Roger Ebert for his inspirational decency and commitment to cinema.

My St. Louis–based research associates included Bob Rust, Cliff Froehlich, Chris Clark, Mike Steinberg, Harman Moseley, Laura Resnick, Brian Ross, and Pete Maniscalco's team at Allied Integrated Marketing.

My informants in Hollywood included Tom Bell, Jack Hodges, D. J. Fone, Richard Vincelli, T. Coraghessan Boyle, and Oliver Stone.

Over the long course of this project I received assistance I could not repay from the Arko, Faessel, Flynn, Hughes, Jensen, Joslyn, Kipper, Miller, Moore, Netzer, Rothschild, and Walsma families, and I received advice I could not refuse from the firm of Formato, Corleone, Tattaglia, Barzini & Soprano.

Thanks to everyone at Hullabaloo for the vintage apparel and to Mike "Sport" Murphy for the soundtrack.

I am forever beholden to my family: Wally, Paul, Laura, Anne, Peter, Chris, Gail, Kelly, Ringo, and most of all my mother, Marie Williams, who gave me a key to her priceless movie-book library as soon as I could read.

Finally and foremost, I thank my wife and drive-in theater companion, Kathryn Welch, who is the answer to the cinematic question, "What did you wish for when you threw that rock?" ★